MARGUERITE
CLARK

AMERICA'S
DARLING
OF BROADWAY
AND THE SILENT
SCREEN

By
Curtis Nunn

The Texas Christian University Press
Fort Worth, Texas

First Printing
Copyright© 1981
by Texas Christian University Press
All rights reserved

Library of Congress Cataloging in Publication Data
Nunn, William Curtis, 1908-
    Marguerite Clark: America's darling of Broadway and the
silent screen.
    Bibliography: p. 166
    "The films of Marguerite Clark": p. 169
    Includes index.
    1. Clark, Marguerite, 1883-1940. 2. Actors — United States —
Biography. 3. Moving-picture actors and actresses — United
States — Biography. I. Title.
PN2287.C544N8   792'.028'0924 [B]   81-4178
ISBN 0-912646-69-1 (pbk.)   AACR2

Manufactured in the United States of America

Dedicated to all those who yet preserve at Patterson the Harry P. Williams Memorial Airport which Marguerite Clark Williams endowed and who keep vital the Wedell-Williams Memorial Aviation Museum of Louisiana whose creation she sustained. These were the things, after Harry P. Williams's death, that were dear to her heart.

Acknowledgments

The Hillcrest Foundation, through a considerate grant, made the writing of this biography possible. Frank B. Williams and Betty Williams, nephew and niece of Harry P. Williams, provided reminiscences of value as did Anne C. Brown, who was long with Williams, Incorporated in New Orleans. Others at New Orleans who contributed informational aid were Eleanor Bright Richardson, Janet W. Yancey, Stanton Frazar, Sherwood Clayton, and Zuma Y. Salaun, while at Patterson, Hugh Brown, Anne Riser, and Helen B. Landry assisted as well. De Witt Bodeen, John Howard Griffin, Smith Ballew, and Bob Robison furthered the endeavor by their knowledgeable encouragements. Paul Parham, Mary Charlotte Faris, and Johnoween Gill of the Mary Couts Burnett Library, Texas Christian University, and Collin B. Hamer, Jr., of the New Orleans Public Library all helped in indicating sources. Barbara Humphrys and Emily Siger, Reference Librarians, Motion Picture, Broadcasting, and Recorded Sound Division, the Library of Congress arranged the viewing of *Mrs. Wiggs of the Cabbage Patch*, the only known existing film of Marguerite Clark in the United States. Mrs. Robert M. Pyle efficiently typed the manuscript. And most important of all to him, the author's wife Inez Petsick Nunn heartened his activity.

Contents

Author's Introduction

In the mid-summer of 1914 at the Airdome Theatre in Georgetown, Texas, I saw Marguerite Clark on the screen for the first time. The film was *Wildflower,* and, stumbling barefoot out of that roofless, hard-benched so-called theatre, I knew that the nickel I had spent for admission had been well expended, for — unknown to anyone else in the world — I had discovered the girl of my dreams. I was a pre-adolescent Edgar Allen Poe who had lost his heart to the shadow of Lenore on a flickering screen. Hereafter, I knew, Mary Pickford and Blanche Sweet would have to step aside for her.

When, soon afterward, the fights at school became frequent (at recess we had no organized play, and I was no Jess Willard), I would keep it in my mind that, on the back of my pencil tablet, inside my desk, safely protected from pugilism, was the colored picture of Miss Clark I had cut from a magazine. I wanted to send her a letter requesting a *signed* picture, but I had difficulty in knowing exactly what to write, and my handwriting was notoriously bad. But write her I did, enclosing twenty-five cents in stamps to cover the cost of the picture. The fact that no picture ever came only heightened my interest in Miss Clark, for, being optimistic, I always thought that I would meet her and forthright overcome all obstacles, including the rather extensive difference in our ages.

But Marguerite Clark never came to Texas that I knew of — much less to Austin, the nearest city to my hometown. Over the next seven years, however, I saw nearly all of her films, and, even though the boy who viewed *Wildflower* was an awkward adolescent by the time he saw *Scrambled Wives* in 1921, he was still enamoured. He treasured broken bits of film salvaged from the garbage can behind the Airdome Theatre. One-sheets, stills, and magazine portraits of Marguerite Clark were still tacked to the wall of his father's barn, just above those of William Farnum, Douglas Fairbanks, Sr., Tom Mix, William S. Hart, Mary Pickford, and Mae Murray.

Thus I admired her then, and later, as an adult reviewing her career, I still valued her contribution to America's stage and screen. Between 1914 and 1921 she made 39 films and ranked second only to Mary Pickford in the hearts of American movie-goers, but even before her entrance into films Miss Clark was a star on Broadway in both musical comedy and on the legitimate stage. If you believe the critics, this elfin actress with the auburn hair and hazel eyes never gave a bad performance and consistently outshone the vehicles in which she was cast. Competence, enthusiasm, and sincerity seem to have marked everything she did, and I despaired that the memory of her contribution was in danger of being lost to the dust of time.

Fortunately, as a professional historian, I was in a position to do something about this contingency, and I was only too happy to leave the battlefields of the Civil War to do it. So, this is a labor of love, written by a man who is anxious to see the history of America's entertainment world preserved, especially insofar as it encompasses the memory of Marguerite Clark, and of those days when we glorified the beautiful, the youthful, and the completely innocent — the heroine whose virtue was never, for the slightest moment, under suspicion — even by the villain.

* * *

Sadly, during the course of my research on this book, only two of Marguerite Clark's films have come to light. *Mrs. Wiggs of the Cabbage Patch* is in the Motion Picture Section of the Library of Congress in Washington, D.C., and a print of the negative has only recently been made. *Silks and Satins* is in the archives of the British Film Institute at London. It is rumored that a print of *Prunella,* frequently considered to be the best of her motion pictures, is somewhere behind the Iron Curtain. Hopefully the publication of this book will stir the waters and bring other extant prints to the surface. If not, it is a pity, for a still photograph can convey only a shadow of the vitality and grace which characterized her performances.

"Thoughtless of beauty,
she was Beauty's self."
Thomson, "Seasons"

PART I

COMIC OPERA
& LEGITIMATE
STAGE

elen Marguerite Clark was born on February 22, 1883, the third child of Helen and Augustus "Gus" Clark, an ambitious haberdasher whose place of business was "located on the prominent downtown corner of Fourth and Walnut in the heart of Cincinnati, the Queen City of Ohio and the valley." At that time Cincinnati was a prosperous city of 250,000 with pretentions to culture; it stood on two terraces above the Ohio River, protected on its landward side by a sweeping semi-circle of high hills. The guide books pointed out its "great schools of art and music; the costly public buildings and the numerous interesting churches and colleges; the great bridges to the Kentucky shore; the inclined-plane railways, climbing sharply to extensive beer-gardens on the hilltops; the beautiful surrounding parks—Eden, Burnet, Woods, and others."

By the time Helen Marguerite was nine years old, the citizens of Cincinnati could pride themselves upon the "Great Exposition Building and Music Hall; the massive and noble edifice of the Chamber of Commerce; the populous German Quarter; the magnificent Tyler-Davidson fountain with its many bronze statues; and the charming highland suburbs of Clifton, Walnut Hills, and others." Among the "others" was flourishing Avondale where "Gus" Clark and his frail wife, Helen, chose to raise their family which, at that time, consisted of Cora, their level-headed oldest daughter; their son, Clifton; and their youngest, Helen Marguerite—the beautiful child.

Downtown, "in the heart of Cincinnati," Clark's haberdashery was located not far from the famous St. Nicholas Restaurant and Hotel of which it was said: "What the Café Bignon is to Paris, the Cafe Savoy to London, Young's to Boston, and Delmonico's to New York, the St. Nicholas is to Cincinnati. No city west of New York has a more deservedly famous restaurant." "Gus" Clark's store evidently appealed to the same clientele, for it prospered until the stable years of the eighties gave way to the hard times of the early nineties. In the depression that moved glacially over the nation in the wake of the financial panic of 1893, "Gus" Clark suffered along with other businessmen in Cincinnati and across the nation.[1]

Then, when Helen Marguerite was almost ten, personal tragedy struck as well. Gentle Helen Elizabeth Clark died on January 21, 1893. Helen Marguerite and the other two Clark children endured this tragedy only to watch their father's business collapse and then to see him become ill of a fatal but lingering illness. Augustus James Clark died on December 29, 1896.

Probate records indicated that Helen Marguerite was almost fourteen at the time of her father's death and that Augustus James Clark left her about four thousand dollars as her portion of the estate. The judge of the probate court named twenty-five-year-old Cora, who had already been serving as manager of the Clark household, as guardian of Helen Marguerite.[2]

Helen Marguerite attended the local public schools, but upon the death of Augustus James Clark, or shortly before, Cora placed her sister in the convent school of the Brown County Ursulines in St. Martin, Ohio. "I was left in the care of my sister," Marguerite Clark wrote years later, having long ago dropped the name of Helen. "I doubt if many parentless children are supplied with as happy and satisfying a substitute as I received. They tell me that the army of chorus girls who come from the F.F.V.'s is the largest in the world, unless it is outnumbered by the stars who began their dramatic careers in a convent. But my first aptitude for the stage *did* display itself during the three years which I spent at the Ursuline convent in Ohio."

None of Marguerite Clark's family had ever appeared upon the stage professionally, and she had no thought of becoming an actress when her first experience before a curtain occurred. Marguerite subsequently wrote of this experience:

One afternoon, I was sent with a message to the sister who was rehearsing some of the older girls in a play. It happened that the play was one from the convent library with which I was familiar, and when I arrived the leading lady was stumbling very badly over her lines. Ordinarily, I was shy and would never have dreamt of speaking to any of the older girls, so imagine their surprise, as well as my own, when I heard myself suddenly piping up, not only with the forgotten lines, but the proper accompanying business as well.

Whether the girl refused to play after that, I don't remember, but the sisters' reproving suggestion that perhaps they would have to let "little Marguerite have the part" was carried out, and I played the leading role. That was the beginning, and after that I was

usually given the leading parts for lack of any one else to do them, I suppose.

This first display of dramatic aptitude must have greatly altered the sisters' opinions of Marguerite as she said of herself that up to that time "I have always been fond of reading, and literally lived in a fairy-world, curled up in a corner of the convent garden when I should have been playing and exercising with the other girls." Even then, she dreamed that her "day —would—come." But with Marguerite's appearance on their stage the sisters discovered that her lyrical singing voice easily carried throughout the main auditorium while her refreshing personality and easy grace in movement would draw audiences to her.

The sisters appreciated her abilities and encouraged her, while Cora, still her legal guardian, and in many ways her shrewd guardian angel with a money-making sense, decided that Marguerite's singing and acting talents would earn them both a good living, and Cora herself would manage the career of Marguerite. Yet Marguerite, according to her own statement, made the final decision alone to turn to the stage as a profession. "I realized, I think, the years of work and struggle and disappointment ahead of me if no success should ever be mine—and realized this to a greater extent, perhaps, than most novices do—still my ambition for a stage career shaped itself quite definitely before I was fifteen, and upon leaving the convent, I came to New York to study with this end in view."

Thus Marguerite Clark, weighing scarcely ninety pounds and possessing only four feet ten inches in height, braved New York, chaperoned and guarded, and soon to be managed by her ambitious though practical sister. New York, the great theater center of the nation, should be, they decided, where Marguerite's opportunities for the stage would open. A brief period of dramatic school training followed, concluded by a production wherein she appeared and for which she received a certificate from the school.

About the time Marguerite Clark was completing her brief dramatic school training, she played in another amateur production, and there, according to Marguerite, "Milton Aborn chanced to see me and offered me my first chance—a position in the chorus of his opera company. Thus I made my debut with him in Baltimore, Maryland," for she accepted the position "acting on the advice of my friend Clara Lane and her husband J. K. Murray." J. K. Murray and Clara Lane were Aborn's stars. Marguerite's principal duties consisted of shouting, "Oh here come the soldiers" in *Maritana* and acting the role of a dumb page in *Fra Diavolo*. Milton Aborn managed the Strakosch Opera Company in Baltimore, and there she spent part of the year 1899, writing of it later, "I remained with the company for several months and then went to New York."[3]

One season in Baltimore was enough. Ambitious Cora whisked Marguerite off to New York where she put a new motor into opportunity before it could develop a knock. She quickly obtained Marguerite a position, and, according to Marguerite's statement, "I was engaged as understudy for several of the principal singing parts of George W. Lederer's company in *The Belle of Bohemia* at the Casino. Several times I was also to play the lead." There was a pleasant side to all of this for "an unknown admirer was sending me flowers at every performance."

The method Cora and Marguerite used in landing the singing part as chorus girl and understudy to Irene Bentley in *The Belle of Bohemia* was simple, as Marguerite wrote: "My sister and I never took 'No' for an answer. When we were told a producer was out, we just waited around until he came in." Then she gave an example. "The day I first met Mr. Frohman we tipped the elevator boy in the Empire building, and he told us how to waylay him. We had never seen him before, and when he came the boy whispered, 'there he is.'" Marguerite remained unperturbed. "I just walked up as though I had known him for years and

said, 'How-d'ye-do, Mr. Frohman?' He couldn't remember ever having set eyes on me before, but although he was puzzled he took it for granted we had met. He had no part to offer me, but sent me over to Mr. Dillingham. I always followed the very simple policy—persistence and patience."

She used the persistence and patience approach successfully and said "For the next twelve seasons it was only during the briefest intervals that I was one of the unemployed. Of course this was largely due to good luck, and it is nothing to boast of."

"The following year I was in the 'The Burgomaster' and the 'The New Yorkers.'" Success began to nod slightly toward her in that season of 1901 when *Broadway Magazine* approved of her and wrote, "Miss Clark has been the hit of 'The Burgomaster' company playing at the Tremont Theater in Boston." She also played the soubrette in that musical comedy in New York, and then, immediately afterwards, appeared in another comic opera with Dan Daly, 'The New Yorkers', at the Herald Square theater where her solo "Oh, So Coy" gained favorable attention. Critics remarked on "so much talent being wrapped up in so winsome and diminutive a package."[4]

The year 1902 proved to be a more satisfactory year to Marguerite Clark. By early May, she was appearing in a Broadway musical comedy titled *The Wild Rose* in which Eddie Foy starred. Irene Bentley, described by the *New York Times* as "piquant and comely," again played the feminine lead. Marguerite was cast in a male role as Lieutenant Gaston Ordannes—a very young and girlish officer. Also appearing in the comedy was beautiful, dark-haired Evelyn Nesbit who years later became the center of front page sensational stories after Harry Thaw, her wealthy husband, allegedly murdered Sanford White, a famous architect, because of White's supposedly romantic attentions to her.

George Jean Nathan, New York dramatic critic writing in 1920, remembered *The Wild Rose* of 1902

and recalled too the producer George W. Lederer as "the American papa of the so-called revue" and "world papa of the so-called girl show"—and Lederer's part in creating that "girl show" *The Wild Rose.* "Think of that galaxy he turned loose in a single evening in the famous *Wild Rose,* probably the most notable collection of pretty women a single stage ever disclosed." And Nathan continued listing his "galaxy" as follows:

Irene Bentley, the most beautiful music show luminary of her day: a dazzling blonde girl with a complexion like a blushing charlotte russe and a mouth like an apricot that had just had its feelings hurt. Little Marie George with the pert brown curls (what movie material there was in those movieless days) and the saucy beauty spot upon the right cheek. Evelyn Nesbit, then a youngster just from Pittsburgh. Edna Hunter, with that peculiar expression of always looking homesick, ever attractive to men. Marguerite Clark, Elsie Ferguson, Elba Kenny, the celebrated Viola Carlstedt, Neva Aymer, Mazie Follette, Belva Don Kersley, Teddie du Coe, Hazel Manchester, Mabel Power, Nina Randall, Jessie Jordan, Irene Bishop. . . there were others, but memory cannot retain completely so rich a treasury.[5]

The musical comedy ran for weeks during the early summer of 1902 at the Knickerbocker Theatre, on Broadway and 38th Streets. The Knickerbocker advertised it in the *New York Times* as a "stunning big jollity hit," and the same announcement declared that the *New York Herald* wrote of "bursts of applause"; the *New York Sun* announced that "Eddie Foy tickled the audience immensely—should run all summer"; and the *World* said that it "has songs that will be played on every piano." The critic of the *New York Times* found that the star "Mr. Eddie Foy appears in one of those eccentric parts which give him plenty of opportunity for the display of his peculiar

characteristics . . . The dancing is generally good, and the singing is equal to the demands of the music. The entertainment will probably have a prosperous career."[6]

Marguerite was ambitious in 1902. "I owe everything in the world to my size," announced the little singer-actress of the *Wild Rose* company, as she stood in the wings of the Knickerbocker Theatre one night in May, 1902, while trying to smooth out an imaginary wrinkle in her faultlessly fitting red tights. "Mr. Lederer took me when I had nothing to recommend me but my voice. He saw me in *The Burgomaster* first and gave me a chance in New York with Mr. Daly in *The New Yorkers,* and now for the second time he has let me have a part that just fits me almost as well as this lieutenant's uniform." Concerning her size, she was modest but confident: "I only weigh ninety-six pounds, you know, and am but four feet nine inches tall, so you see it is not the easiest thing in the world to fit me with a part. But once I have one, and make a hit in it, I feel perfectly secure, for there are very few who are able to successfully understudy me. Then, too, I have lots of time." She admitted to be "only 17 years old" in 1902, although the Probate Court records in Cincinnati assessed her with two more birthdays than that. "I study as hard in my own way to perfect myself for whatever part I may get in musical comedy, as any Shakespearian actor ever did. Every hour in my day has its work, duty, or pleasure. I take an hour's walk through the park every morning before breakfast, have a dancing lesson immediately after work, from there I go to my gymnasium, where I exercise for half an hour with the foils, a plunge, and then luncheon. Three afternoons a week I have my singing lesson, and when I have nothing else to do, I memorize poetry, for I have to become what is known in the profession as a 'quick study.'"[7]

The interview occurred in May in the budding days of the *Wild Rose,* but the musical comedy still brightly lingered on the stem in August, 1902, when tiny Marguerite created temporary havoc with her French heels as she accidentally but effectively trod on the foot of the giant comedian, Al Hart, one of the featured entertainers. A New York reporter recorded the gory details:

"Ouch! oh, my foot! my foot!"
Al Hart's voice echoed through the corridors of the Knickerbocker Theatre Building shortly before matinee hour yesterday afternoon like the roar of a maddened bull.

"I'm killed! I'm dying!" he shrieked, and grabbing his right foot, he did one of those hop dances which comedians frequently execute to a staccato movement of the bass drum. Stage hands, actors, chorus girls, people from offices, and a small battalion of newsboys rushed from all quarters and gathered about the gigantic comedian.

Hart weighs 198 pounds. At his side stood Marguerite Clark, the tiny comedienne of "The Wild Rose." With tears of sympathy, the dainty little woman stood at the giant's side attempting to assuage his grief.

It was a touching scene, fit to inspire the motif for a bill poster. Hart, six feet two inches in height calling his pain to Heaven, and Miss Clark, who is hardly a handful, standing by and imploring him to be brave. Mob in background gazing open eyed.

"What's the row?" asked George Lederer whose attention had been attracted by the immense number of people scattered around the stage entrance.

Hart rolled his eyes and tried in vain to explain.

"Can't some one speak? Can't some one tell me what's the matter with Al Hart, asked Mr. Lederer.

"Yes, sir," said Miss Clark. "I accidentally stepped on his toe."

"Is that all," asked Mr. Lederer.

"Is that all?" exclaimed Hart. "Isn't that enough?"

"Surely, it isn't enough to make a row about. Why, Miss Clark only weighs eighty-two pounds."

"That's all right." said Hart, who was still nursing his injured foot. "I didn't say she weighed a great deal; but look at those French heels—sharp. Now, how would you like to be stabbed in the foot with one of those heels propelled by eighty-two pounds?"

Hart turned away indignantly and took the elevator to his dressing room. Then he painfully shed his shoe. Immediately the foot began to swell, and so quickly that in a moment the injured member had assumed an abnormal size and he was unable to draw on the boot which he wears with the gypsy costume.

Eddie Foy happened by and kindly offered assistance. Hart laid back on a couch and gritted his teeth while Eddie played bootjack.

After a death struggle Foy emerged triumphant and bowed appreciatively to a nearby mirror. Then he suddenly noticed that he had placed the left boot on Hart's right foot. He departed quietly without waiting developments.

When Hart made the discovery of Foy's villainy, he screamed again and said that he would not go on the stage. The Lederers were sent for. It was nigh time for Hart's cue. The wrong boot was quickly pulled from the right foot and he was told to hustle. He stood up, but could not walk without limping painfully.

Every one was in a quandary, and it was finally decided to have Joe Sullivan, assistant stage manager at the Knickerbocker, and Hart's understudy, attempt the part. After a lightning change of costume, Sullivan emerged from the flies barely in time to save the performance from a hitch.

He did the part very well and reappeared at the performance last night. [8]

De Wolf Hopper doubtless noticed in *The Wild Rose* the grace, beauty, and singing ability of Marguerite Clark, for before the year was over she was playing the featured role of Polly in *Mr. Pickwick*, a musical comedy starring the tall, bald, and very popular Hopper.[9] The comic opera, remotely based on Charles Dickens's *Pickwick Papers* opened on January 19, 1903, at the Herald Square Theatre on Broadway and 35th Streets. Manuel Klein composed the music; Charles Klein wrote the book, while the lyrics were from the pen of Grant Stewart.

After opening night, the *New York Times* wrote of De Wolf Hopper in the leading role:

This Mr. Pickwick had a deep and gutteral voice and a decidedly wabbling walk; he made grimaces, and frequently laughed at his own antics. He was a familiar personage to most of those present, for this Mr. Pickwick was just the same De Wolf Hopper of old, resorting to his familiar methods to induce some show of merriment from his audience. The "Mr. Pickwick" of the Messrs. Klein, aided and abetted by Grant Stewart, is just plain every day comic opera—as the term has come to be understood.

It is not without some elements of a broadly amusing sort, and its music is sufficiently familiar to ring pleasantly in the ears. Its best accomplishments are those of the costumer and scene painter . . . What is best of Dickens is not for the theatre—certainly not for the comic opera stage.[10]

Mr. Pickwick, described by the *Sun* as "wholesome and clean" and carrying advertisements in the *New York Times* lauding itself as being "a genuine novelty and a distinctive treat for men and women of discriminating tastes," lasted for about two months. The *Times* declared on March 15 that "De Wolf Hopper will begin his last week at the Herald Square Theatre in *Mr. Pickwick* tomorrow night. Then the company will go on the road. It is announced that the same attraction will be offered again next season."[11]

Marguerite Clark, managed and well chaperoned by capable Cora, went on the road with *Mr. Pickwick*. Life on the road could be exciting, but it promised long and sometimes coal-smoked train rides, drafty hotel rooms, and dining car and restaurant menus that

varied all too greatly in quality. Home became wherever *Mr. Pickwick* played for the night or nights.

Other New York newspapers were kinder to *Mr. Pickwick* than the *Times*. One of them wrote of "the tumultuous welcome accorded to Mr. Hopper" and added that "Mr. Hopper's *Mr. Pickwick* will appeal to those who like snappy lyrics, catchy tunes and wit that jabs you like an uppercut . . . Mr. Hopper seems to have inserted a few new keys in his upper register, for he sang better than at any time since the days of *Wang*." The account praised Marguerite Clark and noted:

Next to Mr. Hopper, tiny Marguerite Clark, as Polly, scored the hit of the night in a song called "Acting," in which she essays the roles of all the actors in a conventional melodrama, and at the end as the heroine falls in a faint to be revived by the Apollolike hero who seems to be carried in stock for all deserving working girls. That fall last night caught the house, and Miss Clark, like Mr. Hopper, is assured of chops and tomato sauce a la Broadway for some time to come.

Between the first and second acts of *Mr. Pickwick*, De Wolf Hopper, already popular in New York for his *Casey at the Bat*, made a sad-faced but witty speech in which he thanked the audience for "fifty per cent of commendation," and pathetically appealed to it to keep him in New York and spare him indigestion. "Tired of the lunch wagons in Lynchburg, Painted Post, and Chicago, you know."[12]

On the road at Chicago with the *Mr. Pickwick* cast, Marguerite had an unexpected honor conferred upon her. She wrote of the occasion years later, in 1913, for the *Chicago Herald*:

An experience that I shall always remember came to me while I was appearing as Polly. Governor Sayers of Texas gave me the appointment of special representative of the Lone Star State in the International Live Stock Exposition at the stockyards.

A special bronze medal was designed for me and presented to me at the exposition.

Then the newspaper continued the account, which though stated to be hers sounded unlike Marguerite and the three years alluded to here could hardly have occurred in her early life without having been known or mentioned by others. It either happened as she wrote it, or an imaginative reporter, for lack of sufficient copy, created the tale himself as publicity for Marguerite. The story follows:

Three years of my life were spent on the ranch of Colonel Robert C. Sanderson at Big Spring, Texas, and I became an experienced ranch woman. There I learned to ride bucking broncos and to use the lariat like a cowboy.[13]

After *Mr. Pickwick* there followed a brief experience of singing in Victor Herbert's *Babes in Toyland* when she played the role of Contrary Mary, leaving De Wolf Hopper's company for six weeks to do so.

Then in July, 1903, at the Crystal Gardens atop of the New York Theatre, George W. Lederer presented her as Rosie Dawn, champion long distance Geisha in the farcical *The Darling of the Gallery Gods* "where she had a part specially written into the burlesque for her," and appeared by special arrangement with De Wolf Hopper. Burlesque carried a more refined meaning in those days. "She will not lose anything by contact with the other women in the cast," wrote a New York reporter. "Her methods, I think, are much more dainty and attractive than any of them." On the same evenings at the Crystal Gardens, Marguerite appeared briefly in the "travesty," *The Dress Parade*, in which she played her old part of Polly from *Mr. Pickwick* and was given a scene with William W. Black, whose make-up as Hopper playing the Dickens character has won favorable mention."

Sam Shubert and William A. Brady, in early August, 1903, engaged Marguerite Clark to play the role of Mataya in support of De Wolf Hopper in *Wang* for

"the coming season." The *New York Telegraph* commented: "Little Miss Clark was a member of Mr. Hopper's company for two seasons and scored quite a hit in support of the tall comedian. She is very tiny herself but very pretty and artistic with a good singing voice."[14]

De Wolf Hopper appreciated her charm and singing talents as he placed Marguerite in a leading role in *Happyland* in 1905. On Monday evening, October 2, Hopper opened in New York at the Lyric Theatre in the new comic opera *Happyland*, and the piece had already received the commendation of Boston and the road. Marguerite Clark, in the role of Sylvia, awaited the verdict of New York with great anticipation.

In its Tuesday paper the *Times* announced of *Happyland*: "It pleases — song hits — rich pictures." Then the same newspaper report detailed: "De Wolf returned to New York last night. That is equivalent to saying that for some weeks to come the number of places where people may go and laugh will be augmented by one. For there is little doubt that the comedian's new vehicle will be to the liking of the people who like him. The number of such persons happens to be considerable." The paper thought that Frederic Rankin, the author of the book, and Reginald De Koven, the composer of the musical score should be jubilant as well. "Its music is agreeable, and there are several numbers that will probably be whistled and sung all over town in a week."

As to the plot, the *Times* narrated:

Mr. Hopper, as the King of Elysia, suddenly makes the outstanding discovery that married people are never happy, and as he has grown tired of being always happy himself and seeing nothing but happiness about him, he arranges for marriages for all the men and women of his court . . .

The monarch of Elysia has promised that his son shall marry the daughter of a neighboring monarch. But as he has no son, as may be surmised, he now determines *to pass his daughter off as a boy. But here the librettist does make a departure.*

The girl runs away before her father has carried out his purpose. In consequence, the monarch suddenly discovers that life, even in Elysia, was not all one sweet song. It is not necessary to go into further details.

The critic of the *New York Times* summarized the star's contributions: "Mr. Hopper in his broad, low comedy way manages to extract a great deal of fun from the various complications that follow. In this, he has excellent assistance in William Danforth, who appears as the other monarch." Then the critic of the *Times* turned in praise to Marguerite: "And in Marguerite Clark a dainty wisp of a woman who dances through several scores like a being from fairyland."[15]

The *New York Globe* described the opening night enthusiastically and said of the leading lady: "Marguerite Clark, a pretty, graceful, sweet-voiced girl who as Sylvia, daughter of King Estaticus . . . was quite the hit of the production . . . The audience was with her from start to finish, and whether New York likes *Happyland* or not, there is no doubting the fact that the theatre public will rejoice over a pretty girl who can sing prettily, speak prettily, and who never once reminds you of the music halls." At the same time, Channing Pollock commented: "She has become quite the most popular woman in comic opera on Broadway." And he added, "The Shuberts have signed a five-year contract with her, guaranteeing a stellar engagement at the end of that period of time."[16]

Marguerite Clark had advanced a bit more on the road toward stardom, and *Happyland*, a music comedy hit, remained at the Lyric the rest of the year. De Wolf Hopper then took *Happyland* on the road, as he was crowded out of the Lyric "to make room for Sarah Bernhardt." Marguerite continued to play the role of Sylvia in the comic opera and went on the road

with the cast, where she sometimes faced audiences that differed indeed in size and reception from those who had viewed the show in New York. At Petersburg, Virginia, where the actors in *Happyland* spent one night while on the road, De Wolf Hopper reported that "The people of that place were no doubt very nice, but I really don't know—there were so few of them."[17]

Life on the road carried its discomforts, and Marguerite wrote of its hardships. "I loved it at first," she noted a few years later, "but that soon wears off. And then when the edge of novelty goes, the ceaseless travel becomes a nightmare—miserable hotels, bad food; cold cars; up and out of bed at dawn to catch trains (because the night stand falls to all beginners and they must go through its lengthy ordeal); no time for relaxation, little time to take care of one's health; no new faces, but the same old persons to talk to day in and day out—in short a gypsy life without a dash of color, without the vaguest tinge of romance.

"Even in later years after the hard years of apprenticeship, there come months of this sort of thing. The period of stay in the larger cities is variable and fickle, and the road must be resorted to in the endless campaign for financial gain. Even after success comes, that dreaded nightmare of travel haunts the actress. She has no place she may call home. She no sooner gets settled in a place than off she must go. And this holds for the most famous star as it does for the lowliest little chorus girl."[18]

De Wolf Hopper brought *Happyland* back to New York and reopened it at the Casino Theatre, again with the same cast, in March, 1906. Marguerite continued to gain much praise as Princess Sylvia. "Marguerite Clark as the king's daughter in De Wolf Hopper's *Happyland* almost ran away with the honors during the successful presentation of the Shubert comedy." Thus wrote *Bob Taylor's Magazine* in April, 1906, and continued:

Marguerite Clark, as De Wolf Hopper's leading lady in *Happyland*.

At left, Marguerite Clark, in *Happy-land*, received much favorable attention by the press.

DeWolf Hopper, above, a reigning king of musical comedy in 1905, starred on Broadway in the hit *Happyland*.

This miniature prima donna danced her way into the hearts of the audiences and then entranced them further with her really charmingly cultivated voice. She is as winsome and graceful as a wild rose blossoming in the fields of fairyland, and so guileless of mien that you are ready to believe that she is really the artless little princess she purports to be.[19]

Most of the cities over the country enthusiastically received *Happyland*—and Marguerite Clark. Charles Howard in the *New York Globe* wrote that she "is without a counterpart among soubrettes for the tiny loveliness of her person. She sings and dances with fairy art." And the *Boston Transcript* wrote of her that she seemed "like a childish Juliet" and was "the embodiment of youthful innocence and girlish grace. For such a tiny creature her voice is remarkable, and she apparently has striven intelligently to make the most of it. Throughout she is delightful."[20]

Always Cora went with Marguerite on the road. She packed Marguerite's trunks, went to the theatre with her as she did in New York, and looked after "all her affairs." "All that I have to do," said Marguerite, "is to come to the theatre and do the best I can. I'm in bed every night by half-past twelve."[21] Cora was with her in Cincinnati when their home city's newspaper took Marguerite to its heart, calling her "Pretty Marguerite Clark prima donna in Happyland," and then telling in detail of a reported romance, saying that she "was seen last night at the Hotel Havlin with Melville Ellis, who is connected with the Shuberts and whose name has been mentioned with Miss Clark in a possible matrimonial venture of the near future." The *Enquirer* elaborated that the couple, "with Miss Clark's sister," had been asked if there was any truth in the report. The question had been put as the three were leaving the hotel dining room followed by "servants bearing floral offerings that had been received by the prima donna in her first visit to her home city."

"I hope," Marguerite answered evasively, "that you are not after as lurid an article as when I fell in the Avondale Athletic Club pool and was rescued some years ago. Here's Mr. Ellis right at my side. Ask him."

"Ellis," said the *Enquirer*, "answered with the promptitude of a true knight. 'I have told Miss Clark that I will be ready whenever she is, and I am ready now.' "

Marguerite then hastily interposed. "No, there is no truth in it. Mr. Ellis and I are just good friends. We have had a good joke together. Every time he meets me he asks 'When are we to be married, Marguerite?' And I answer, 'When we meet in Poughkeepsie.' And don't you know we have never as yet met in Poughkeepsie."

" 'Well, we will some day,' answered Mr. Ellis."

" 'You can say for me,' said Miss Clark 'that both of us intend to get married some day, but I can't say we are going to wed each other.' "

" 'Well, we will if I have my way,' " answered Mr. Ellis as he stepped on the elevator.[22]

There was never any rendezvous at Poughkeepsie. Marguerite continued to sing her way over much of America in *Happyland*, while Melville Ellis evidently retained his connection with the Shuberts somewhere else. Anyway the alleged romance may have originated with the Shuberts in their efforts to create publicity for their miniature "Lyric Cameo"—as one of her journalistic admirers called Marguerite.

In an interview in March 1906, she told of her early struggles and said, "Talk about the exhaustion of climbing stairs! There are a thousand steps between the chorus and the cast, and every one of them has to be mounted with toil and trouble. All the while I was playing small parts, I took singing lessons, and a dozen other kinds of lessons. I used to study the parts that other people played and to pray selfishly that some one might be taken sick—just a little sick, you know—so that I might have my opportunity. When it did come, I could hardly believe my good fortune. I can liken my experience only to that which I had when, after trying for three years to learn to

swim, I suddenly found myself doing it. I remember that when I looked back at my person floating in the water, I said: 'Are those really my feet.' That was the way I felt about my hit in *Happyland*."[23]

Marguerite received her share of appreciation from the patrons of *Happyland*. But there was an unexpected incident during the Yuletide season of 1905 which made, so she wrote, "that occasion perhaps the happiest of any other Christmas in my recollection." And thus she told the story:

We had been playing at the Lyric three months previously, and every evening on my way to the theatre, I would stop to purchase a paper from one particular blue eyed, curly haired news boy, whose gentle manner and softness of speech had attracted me to him. It was my custom to pay him five cents for the paper instead of a penny which was the regular charge, as I had hoped to encourage a spirit of thrift in this little merchant. I would take occasion to tell him stories of how great fortunes had been founded on the very smallest of savings.

Imagine my surprise when I stepped out of the theater after the Christmas matinee to find my little friend waiting for me. In his arms he carried dozens of rich red roses. It was a bleak day. Snow covered the ground, and everything about, save the pretty picture of this little news chap with his Christmas present of fresh flowers, was cheerless and dispiriting. He approached me, and doffing his ragged cap, he thrust the roses towards me, and in mumbled tones, wished me the compliments of the season. Without further ado, he scampered away.

The suddenness of the whole affair took me with such great surprise that I was unable to thank him. Later I learned the boy had saved all the extra pennies that I had given him above the regular price of the paper until he had enough on hand to purchase the Christmas gift . . . The roses are withered and gone, but the remembrance of their perfume and the kindness which inspired the gift

makes me appreciate this tribute a great deal more than I would had I received a hundred of the rarest exotics from one of the highest dignitaries in the world.[24]

Printed musical numbers were given to the audience as souvenirs at the performance on Wednesday, April 4, to celebrate *Happyland's* "200th time in New York."[25] Later in April, *Happyland* moved from the Casino to the Majestic Theatre on 59th Street. By May, special summer prices were being offered with the best seats at $1.00 for all performances, and Hopper was advertising himself as the star in "his greatest success—with Marguerite Clark."[26] *Happyland* closed in early June, 1906.

Nineteen seven was such a bad time for business over the nation that it has been named a panic year. The theaters on Broadway remained open as usual, but there was no *Happyland* in New York for Marguerite Clark. Still once again De Wolf Hopper took her on the road in it, that time as far west as Milwaukee where she played a half-week's engagement in December, 1907.

Yet in New York, certain stage producers did not forget her. In May, the Shuberts announced that they would present Marguerite in *The Road to Yesterday* at the Waldorf Theatre, London on the legitimate stage "following the engagement of E. H. Sothern and Julia Marlowe." Marguerite had been identified only with musical plays since she began as a chorus girl some years before, and although it was known that the Shuberts expected eventually to place her at the head of a company, the *New York Telegraph* wrote that no one had suspected her transfer to the "legitimate." Four months later, the *New York Times* wrote that "among those who have been thus promoted into luminary prominence" by the Shuberts "are Miss Marguerite Clark who has heretofore been the principal comedienne with De Wolfe Hopper, but whose name will hereafter be blazoned forth in

electric lights as the star of a new play by Rida Johnson Young."[27]

Marguerite Clark was destined to become a star of the legitimate theater later—but not in 1907. Still Meigs O. Frost, a New Orleans friend of hers, enthusiastically recalled years later for the *Times-Picayune* the days in 1907 and 1908 when he saw her on Broadway:

She was a slim little thing with an ivory and rose skin, with hair of pure bronze, and she was absolutely the toast of Broadway. She had a sister we used to call the Dragon because she was such an effective chaperone.

Never the faintest hint of scandal ever touched her. She never went in for champagne parties, and if any one sent her diamonds, she promptly sent them back. Every manager who ever knew Marguerite Clark said she was a good trooper. She worked hard and never complained. All theatre employees referred to her as Miss Clark rather than Marguerite because of a certain quiet dignity—not that she was snotty mind you.[28]

The "dragon" chaperone of the early 1900s—the stage mother—in Cora's case, the stage sister, is something unknown today. Such an overzealous guardian twisted the growth of many a budding genius of the footlights, and under the pretense of protecting the gifted one's virtue and managing her affairs, actually limited her development and thwarted romance in her life. But as for Cora, she was wise to be protective, as Marguerite was a tantalizing, though diminutive darling. Her lovely features, auburn hair, and hazel eyes were made doubly attractive by her charm in manner and grace in movement. There was something dainty—like a Dresden doll about her. The press was won over, and she was described as petite, extremely well dressed, and completely feminine. The newspapers liked her dancing and singing abilities when in musical

Miss Clark's portrait for the press in 1909.

comedy, and later they would praise her humor as a comedienne on the legitimate stage and laud her beauty in motion pictures. So in many respects, Cora did well to guard her little sister who was such an enchanting, delightful, though constant ingenue.

Marguerite valued the enthusiastic protection Cora provided, and if any romances of hers were thwarted by the older sister, at least Marguerite's list of performances did not include playing Red Riding Hood opposite any bright-eyed, stage-door wolf. "You will not be able to take care of yourself as well as you think if you take up the life of the theater," she once confided to the *Chicago Record* and continued:

Unless you have a mother, or brother, or sister, or someone to look out for you, you are destined to have a great deal of trouble. In their commendable desire not to seem slingers of mud against their calling, my sisters of the stage have permitted themselves to fib somewhat about temptation in the life of the stage. Their not entirely true statements are to be pardoned for the reason cited; but the fact, the grim fact remains that the truth ought to be told.

The theater is full of temptations for the young girl. I do not believe I am doing wrong in saying so because other professions as well are probably not entirely devoid of temptation. This is not a pleasant subject, and need not be gone into in detail; but I do want to impress all these little girls, who think the stage is the place for them, with the truth of the situation. If any one tells you there is no temptation in the theater, he is leading you into error. It is silly to attempt to deny what exists. In no circumstances, should a young girl enter into the life of the theater without someone to protect her and watch out for her. The theater is a great, grand, splendid institution; but as in most great institutions, one finds spiders which spin their alluring, deadly webs. And these webs are often not so far a way up in the rafters.[29]

De Wolf Hopper was not one to let New York forget him. He revived *Wang*, a travesty of *The Mikado*, which he had first introduced in 1904; and Marguerite Clark had the featured role in it. After that, he opened as the star in the *Pied Piper*, "a new musical piece by Strong, Burnside, and Klein," at the Majestic Theatre on December 3, 1908. Below his capitalized name in the starring role in the *Pied Piper*, De Wolf Hopper announced in the same advertisement that Marguerite Clark was "Specially Engaged."[30]

As to the opening night with Hopper in the role of the *Pied Piper*, the *Times* commented: "The piece is the usual Broadway comic opera type with lively dances and bright songs. Mr. Hopper, in his own familiar vein, makes the most of everything and manages to keep his audience in continuous merriment. Mr. Hopper has with him again this year little Miss Marguerite Clark, the graceful dancer."

The *Times* then turned to the music:

Some of the songs which evoked the heartiest applause were "Woman's a Wonderful Thing" by Mr. Hopper; "Adam and Eve" by Miss Grace Cannon, "I'm Looking for a Sweetheart" by Miss Marguerite Clark and John Phillips; "It's the Little Things That Count in Life" by Miss Cameron and "It Really Was a Very Pretty Story" by Miss Clark.[31]

Alan Dale, a New York critic of that time, was quoted as writing: "The *Pied Piper* for mine any day as an alternative for the typical Broadway Show. Hopper is a host in himself. He was let loose among the cute little kids in the City of Innocence and was the biggest kid of them all." The New York *Herald* announced that a "crowded house applauded at every opportunity."[32]

De Wolf Hopper and Marguerite Clark in the musical comedy *The Pied Piper* (1908).

At right, Marguerite Clark in the leading role of *The Beauty Spot* (1909).

Below, according to the New York Times, there was "plenty of dash and ginger" in *The Beauty Spot* (1909).

Marguerite Clark left a successful run of the *Pied Piper* to appear in the leading role of Nadine in the *Beauty Spot* with Jefferson de Angelis as the star. The musical comedy opened in New York at the Herald Square Theatre on April 10, 1909, and the *New York Times* wrote of the show that:

It is one of those aimless combinations of hurrah and hosiery that usually sprout with the spring and continue to tra la when the days grow longer and hotter. Of its kind, it is a pretty good sort of a show too with plenty of dash and ginger, pretty girls, and the kind of a story that can mean anything you want it to mean, and will not trouble you if you are not particularly fond of stories told in patches.

Toward the star, Jefferson de Angelis, the *Times* indicated but mild satisfaction, feeling that he was not as entertaining as "the prominence of his name might indicate." "He dances well and he does a song, giving an imitation of a man in a cinematograph which is very funny." Then the *Times* admitted that "also he succeeds in accomplishing the remarkable feat of singing 'She Sells Sea Shells by the Sea Shore' without getting his lips tied up, but the greater part of the time he is hopelessly engaged in trying to make material funny which isn't funny on its own account and to which his efforts lend no humor."

Still the critic in the *Times* was pleased with Marguerite. "Marguerite Clark dances and sings her way through the piece charmingly as usual." He was more pleased with Reginald De Koven's music and described it as being "tuneful, bright, soothing, and spirited as the occasion requires. It is, in fact, the best feature of the general performance."[33]

In the summer of 1909, Marguerite, with sister Cora, left New York musicals for a time to head a stock company at the Suburban Garden in St. Louis. There she achieved overnight success with *Peter Pan* the opening play. A St. Louis newspaper wrote: "It was with more than casual interest that a very large audience at the Suburban Garden last night saw some one else than Maude Adams essay Peter Pan." And the paper added: "The some one else was Marguerite Clark, who made as dainty and as romantic a boy as ever fairy smiled upon or pirate ran from or an Indian maiden doted upon."

Marguerite had made her dramatic debut in *Peter Pan*, and her career would no longer ever be confined to musical comedies and light operas. She was showered with flowers and good wishes from people of the theatrical world. There were so many bouquets "that one could not see the tiny star." Two huge bouquets were of "American beauty roses taller than Miss Clark—one from Lee and Sam Shubert and the other from De Wolf Hopper." Floral tributes also came from Jefferson de Angelis, Ralph J. Cohn, Eugene Barrington, Wilton Lackaye and others.[34]

Marguerite recalled on opening night of *Peter Pan* in St. Louis that "At first, I was frightened. The aerial wire was what frightened me. It wasn't put in 'till the last, and then they strung a boy on it to see if it would take the weight, and he was rather badly battered. I had only five minutes practice on the wire—just before the curtain went up, but I came off with all my bones in their regular places, and after that it was easy."[35]

Marguerite followed *Peter Pan* with *The Golden Garter*, at the Suburban Garden, and starred as Zaidee, "a young and innocent Turkish girl" who was adept at disregarding conventions. So successful was the play received that Marguerite and Cora intended to return to summer stock at St. Louis the next season.

The Shuberts still planned a career in legitimate drama for her, and with the coming of fall, Marguerite Clark found herself yet away from New York but starring as Sally in *The Wishing Ring*, a play by Owen Davis, founded on a short story by Dorothea Deakin. The drama opened at the Princess Theatre in Montreal to "a capacity audience" for Marguerite was

"well known here" as having been the leading lady in *Happyland*. A newspaper reported that "congratulatory telegrams from all parts of States were showered upon the popular little comedienne."[36]

By November of 1909, *The Wishing Ring* had reached Chicago. The *Chicago Journal* found that "Miss Clark has a wonderful voice for so small a person, and she reads wonderfully well, because her reading is perfectly natural. She is a very pretty girl too."

The *Journal* continued to praise her acting at the Great Northern Theatre, and said:

Miss Clark gives a very delightful performance, its chief merit resting in her earnestness and her very pronounced and very valuable sense of humor. She is elfin and whimsical, but she softens her spirit of mischief with the spirit of charity. Her make-believe is irresistible, and so is her frankness. We have not in a long time seen the poise of maturity and the exuberance of childhood so skillfully mingled.[37]

Robert Dempster, described by the paper as "a handsome young man," played the supporting role of Giles, the gardener, while Cecil B. DeMille, destined for glory years later as one of the screen's great directors, was the "absent-minded parson who adds to the woes of Sally by his too-broad Christian charity." King Baggott, who would act in leading roles in silent films in the years ahead, was William.[38]

In the last week of November, 1909, Marguerite received notification from Mr. Roth, her business manager, that the Chicago tour in *The Wishing Ring* would "close at the Great Northern Theatre on Saturday night" and that she should prepare to join *The King of Cadonia* company. The musical comedy *The King of Cadonia* "according to the criticisms of the Washington reviewers, is in need of assistance, but Miss Clark, judging from her protests, is unwilling to join the relief party."

Two years before, Marguerite Clark was first mentioned as a prospective Shubert star. During that intervening period, "her talents have been used to bolster up fragile comedies projected to exploit other stars." So the reward of stardom in New York by the Shuberts was somewhat belated, and "now that she has every reason to believe she has registered a fine success in Chicago with *The Wishing Ring*, a legitimate play," she was not accepting kindly the proposed change of activity to a comic opera "in need of assistance." "Of course I like drama best," Marguerite said at about that time. "Every serious-minded theatrical person does. Then next I like comedy like I play in *The Wishing Ring*. But I wouldn't say for anything that I'd never go into musical comedy again. No Sir—ee!"

True she wanted to return to New York and the stardom promised her but in legitimate plays not comic operas. Yet she desired to go back East, for another reason too—the conditions in the Chicago theatre were far from ideal, and Marguerite wrote this to a friend, related the *New York Telegram*:

She has told a story of recent experiences which is harrowing in the details. She says that she and "The Wishing Ring" have established a success in spite of such handicaps as "shop worn scenery, cheap actors, no printing, not a frame of pictures and a canine member of the cast for which the management paid sixty-five cents." She adds that she and Mr. Davis' play are considerably superior as drawing cards to many of the attractions which she has encountered in the theatres of the "Mosquito Trust."[39]

Late in November, newspapers carried a special dispatch from Chicago announcing the marriage of Marguerite Clark to Robert Dempster, leading man in *The Wishing Ring*. The New York *Review* carried the story: "Miss Clark was married last week. She was married secretly. In fact so secretly was the deed done that for several days thereafter no one knew anything about it except Miss Clark, her husband, the minister, and the witnesses of the ceremony. Robert Dempster is the happy man." The dispatch elaborated further, "No musical comedy star has been more popular than Miss Clark. During the several years that she was De Wolf Hopper's leading woman, Miss Clark was as much responsible for the success of his attractions as was Mr. Hopper himself."

The story was a hoax, perhaps circulated by mistaken but well-meaning friends.[40] Marguerite immediately and emphatically denied to the press that she had married Robert Dempster—and as one newspaper put it, "she ought to know." She at once allegedly began an investigation to ascertain how the report started, in order to take strenuous measures to contradict it. Certainly her investigation must have led her toward the Shuberts—Sam and Lee—who were still pressing her to leave the legitimate drama and *The Wishing Ring* in Chicago and return East for stardom in the musical comedy *The King of Cadonia*. They had, once before, created romance—in the case of Melville Ellis in the *Happyland* days—to further publicity for Marguerite.

Practical Marguerite and certainly Cora too—Marguerite's most valued and level-headed adviser—desired publicity, reams of it, but a secret wedding was hardly in the bargain. "There isn't any husband, there hasn't been any husband, and according to weather indications, there isn't going to be any husband for quite some time to come." She told a Chicago reporter for the *Tribune* and added forcefully, "I've never been married in my life." And wheeling right about face and emphasizing with a powder puff, she added the final word, "Never!"

As always, Cora was there to defend her but not one to neglect publicity even on an unfortunate subject. "She never has!" The elder sister was then described by the reporter "as a dainty little person, the all pervading color of whose robes suggested immediately the title of the 'Lavender Lady.'" "She never has!" Cora repeated. "And I think it's such a shame such a report ever got out. Why she never had any thought of marrying Mr. Dempster. Did you dear?"

"Never," Marguerite answered. "You see, I think that I was seen about three times in public with Mr. Dempster. I had lunch and dinner with him several times. Evidently we were seen by some person more romantic than truthful, with the result that we awoke one morning to find ourselves not famous but married. That's the way of it."

"That must have been the way of it," sighed "the Lavender Lady" wearily. "Some of the New York papers corrected the report, and I believe one of the Chicago papers did, but the correction was so small that the correction was not noticed, and Marguerite will always be married in the eyes of some people I suppose."[41]

The Shuberts won, and it was announced in New York by the *Review* on December 5 that Marguerite would become the star of *The King of Cadonia* and Robert Dempster would be included in the cast of the production. Still *The Wishing Ring* would continue its "prosperous career" after the "brilliant little star" had left the company. A few months later, she was asked in New York: "Why did you leave *The Wishing Ring* for *The King of Cadonia* just when you were being discovered as a 'regular human' actress?"

"Manager," she sighed.

"Why didn't you protest?"

"I did protest. I protested fifteen-dollars' worth over long-distance telephone. I begged Mr. Shubert to release me." She did not specify whether he was Sam or Lee Shubert.

"What did he say?"

"If you insist—he said: I won't release you to God."

"Not a trifling compliment."

"No," said Miss Clark. "It cost me $15."[42]

Marguerite Clark described the musical comedy in which she opened as a star at Daly's Theatre in New York during January, 1910, as "the poor, hapless

At right, **Marguerite Clark** as she appeared in her first starring role as Princess Marie in the English musical comedy, *The King of Cadonia*.

Pictured below, **Marguerite Clark** (foreground), as the tiny Princess Marie in *The King of Cadonia*.

MARGUERITE CLARK, WHO STARRED AS PRINCESS MARIE IN THE ENGLISH MUSICAL
COMEDY, "THE KING OF CADONIA"

Marguerite Clark played the featured role of Agnes Ralston in *Jim the Penman*, a melodrama that opened at the Lyric in New York in May, 1910.

'King of Cadonia.'" "Amusing," said the *Times* of the comic opera, as it also announced "Miss Clark's first New York appearance as a full-fledged star," adding that both she and her leading man, William Norris, "shine." Frederic Lonsdale wrote *The King of Cadonia*, Sidney Jones and Jerome D. Kern composed the music, while Adrian Rose and M. E. Rourke penned the lyrics.

Marguerite enacted the role of Princess Marie, and the *New York Times* found that among the "best musical numbers are 'Coo-oo' in which Miss Clark appears with several live turtle doves on her arms and shoulders." During the song "Lena," another of the better numbers, but one in which Princess Marie was not present, "all the comedians rolled over the stage in paroxysms of laughter, which was communicated to the audience."

The *Times* found that the musical comedy "has dash and fun besides tuneful music in plenty," and added:

Around a perfectly palpable plot concerning a king who wasn't loved by his subjects because he kept himself shut up too much, the authors have woven several scenes which serve to display dainty Marguerite Clark in as charming a manner as she has ever been and also to present Mr. Norris at his best. The large audience was manifestly pleased and there were enough encores to keep the audience in their seats until after 11 o'clock.

Still the *Times* noted that the play was marred by a minor accident. "The king in the first act inadvertently lost half of his moustache, which didn't greatly matter, however, as he was shaved a few moments later." The *Theatre Magazine* was enthusiastic and declared:

There is a fine cast . . . each one placed advantageously and all working together at times in positively brilliant ensemble . . . Marguerite Clark bears her new stellar responsibilities with pretty

grace. She is as infantile as ever in face and figure, but she has matured vocally, and is most piquant as the coquettish Princess.[43]

The King of Cadonia did not catch on with the public and reigned briefly at Daly's Theatre on Broadway and 30th Streets. The comic opera was advertised on January 16 with the deadening phrase "Last Eight Times at This Theatre." The same issue of the paper announced that at Daly's on the afternoon of Thursday, January 20, Marguerite Clark would appear as Sally in a special matinee performance of *The Wishing Ring*, a whimsical comedy by Owen Davis.[44] This special appearance produced by the Shuberts marked the first time she had starred in New York in a non-musical play. Yet Marguerite, after experiences with the unfortunate *King of Cadonia*, had no desire for stardom, and she wrote:

And how I hated starring and its responsibilities, even though it meant a mile or two along the road to success! I was at once made to understand that if the house was empty, it was the star's fault not the fault of the play or the weather. If the house was full, the play must be good. If a scene fell down, the star didn't carry it—a slip on the part of any member of the cast could, of course, be traced to the star! Each part, however, with its own particular difficulties, was a stepping-stone for the next, bringing me nearer the work for which I was most happily fitted.[45]

Marguerite Clark forsook musical comedy after the two-week decline and fall of *The King of Cadonia*. She never returned to comic opera and in the spring she appeared in the featured role of Agnes Ralston in *Jim the Penman* which opened in New York at the Lyric Theatre on May 10, 1910. The *New York Times* greeted the play's revival by "Thrills Yet in Jim the Penman, Old Melodrama Acted in Old Time Melodramatic Way at the Lyric Theatre by a Good All Around Cast." The *Times* further commented:

There was no end of enthusiasm at the Lyric Theatre last night where Sir Charles Young's very old-fashioned melodrama of "Jim the Penman" was revived by a so-called "all star" cast in which several of the actors are popular stars. That subsequent performances will arouse as much enthusiasm may well be doubted, as the audience was obviously of the most friendly sort and there was plenty of that kind of first aid to curtain calls which skillful managers know how to use.

"Individually satisfying enough" the *Times* concluded of Marguerite Clark's performance.[46] She had bridged the gulf successfully from comic opera to the legitimate stage.

"People Fighting for Seats Nightly" enthused one advertisement, while J. W. Hamer of the *New York Examiner* was quoted as writing: "Not in years has such a remarkable cast been assembled on any stage." "Will give you any number of starts and make your eyes bulge" wrote an apparently thrill-hungry drama critic for the *New York Evening Mail.*[47]

Jim the Penman may have been the greatest dramatic achievement of Sir Charles L. Young, Bart. of England, but it was too dated to survive long at the Lyric. Marguerite stepped from it to return to summer stock at the Suburban Garden in St. Louis where she starred in *Baby Doll* and had "use for all her skill as an actress, a singer, and a dancer." "It is an ideal summer piece, just the sort of thing to relieve brain fag and," said *Billboard*, "make pessimists believe that things are better than they seem, after all."

On August 23, 1910, she opened at Daly's Theatre as the star of a new hit with the part of Zoie Hardy in *Baby Mine*. "The funniest play that New York has ever seen," praised the *Evening Telegram*, while the *Evening Mail* was enthusiastic but not quite so extensive in regards to the humor in New York's dramatic past and wrote , "The funniest play in 10 years."[48] "*Baby Mine* One Long Lingering Laugh" headlined the *New York Times* and sub-headlined

Scenes from the melodrama, *Jim the Penman*, at the Lyric Theater in New York, 1910.

"Fun of Margaret Mayo's New Farce Cannot Be Imagined. So It Will Be as Well to See It. Convulsed Daly's Audience. Marguerite Clark and Ernest Glendinning Make Hits and Walter Jones Adds Much to Amusement." Enthusiastically, wrote the critic of the *Times*:

Imagine a young wife temporarily estranged from her husband who has caught her in a lie and gone to live in another city to avoid having to see her. Imagine the young wife, at the suggestion of a sympathetic friend, borrowing a baby and sending her husband word that he is a father. Imagine if you can, but you really cannot, so perhaps it will be better to see them, the various complications that result when the mother of the borrowed baby suddenly determines that she must have her offspring back, necessitating the impressing of any other available infant in time to gladden the young father's heart, and imagine the result when instead of finding one baby in the bassinette, the young man finds two and ultimately thinks himself the father of a third.

If you can even approximately imagine all these happenings, you may have some faint idea of the fun in Miss Margaret Mayo's farce "Baby Mine" which literally had people roaring with laughter at Daly's for two hours last night . . . Funny it certainly is—one of the funniest farces this town has ever seen.

Of Marguerite Clark's Zoie, the *Times* wrote:

Incidentally, there is added humor in the attitude of the little wife who doesn't like babies at all and who finds it particularly trying to enthuse over other people's babies, and a pretty touch of tenderness in her disappointment at finding hubby, after his long estrangement, so absorbed in babies that he cannot find time for her.

These more delicate little scenes Miss Marguerite Clark acted with a great deal of winsome charm and sweetness, and the pathetic finish to the first act,

after the husband had rushed angrily away, was done most charmingly. Miss Clark is still the vest pocket bit of humanity, but her grasp of things has broadened vastly. Much that she has to do in the play is childishly acrobatic rather than maturedly histrionic, but wherever the occasion arises in this role for delicacy in acting, she is able to meet it. There is genuine humor too in her playing.[49]

Marguerite originated the role of Zoie Hardy in Chicago, shortly before bringing the play to New York, and there *Baby Mine* ran successfully on Broadway from late August, 1910—past the remainder of the year, "outdistancing the New York runs of all other attractions that started in September."[50]

Marguerite had pleasant memories of the play and recalled, years later in 1918, not only the drama but her association with Sarah Bernhardt at that time:

My first telling work was in "Baby Mine" in which I created the role of Zoie Hardy. At this time, Mme. Bernhardt was playing in a theater near by, and after my performance, I would run to her theater on the chance of seeing her in her dressing-room. Mme. Bernhardt is, to my mind, the greatest actress the world has ever known, and my greatest inspiration. Her portrait as L'Aiglon with the inscription "A Ma Gentile Camarade, Marguerite Clark" is one of my dearest possessions.

After one exceptionally wonderful appearance, I wanted to shower her with roses in sheer gratitude, but every one did that, so I sent her instead a large

Marguerite Clark as Zoie in *Baby Mine*—a hit at Daly's Theatre (1910).

Japanese doll. Imagine my delight when I found her later in her dressing-room surrounded by the most exquisite flowers in the world and hugging my doll in her arms![51]

Baby Mine continued at the Lyric until early 1911, and very shortly after its closing, she was back on the same stage in an entirely different type of play. "Marguerite Clark never seemed more charming and never did better acting than in the role of Shakespeare Jarvis," declared a critic of the *New York Times* concerning her featured role in *Lights O' London*, a revived melodrama produced by William A. Brady during the first week of May, 1911. The old melodrama had originally been played on the London stage in the 1880s, yet the writer of the *Times* felt that on opening night the dated production "acquired sufficient momentum at the very start to carry it probably beyond the four weeks of time alotted to it."

In the cast too appeared Douglas Fairbanks, Sr., Doris Keane, and Holbrook Blinn—all of these—like Marguerite Clark—destined for greater fame.

Marguerite was not the lead in this melodrama and played instead the role of a child—a boy, Shakespeare Jarvis—who is nursed through a serious illness by Bess, the leading feminine character in the play.

On the opening night "there were several incidents not on the program that added to the audience's pleasure" recounted the critic of the *Times*, who added:

In the first place, the curtain went up much too soon and disclosed a crowd of stage hands getting the first scene in order.

Then the lights in Squire Armitage's study refused to be extinguished for the robbery scene, and later the descending curtain cut off a march of "extra" policemen, leaving part of the procession outside of the curtain line. And in the finale of the fourth act, when Harold leaps into the river to rescue Preene,

Upper left, Marguerite Clark and Ernest Glendinning: "*Baby Mine* One Long Lingering Laugh" headlined *The New York Times* in September, 1910.

Lower left, Marguerite Clark and Ernest Glendinning in *Baby Mine* (1910).

Below, Marguerite Clark, Walter Jones, and Ernest Glendinning in *Baby Mine* (1910).

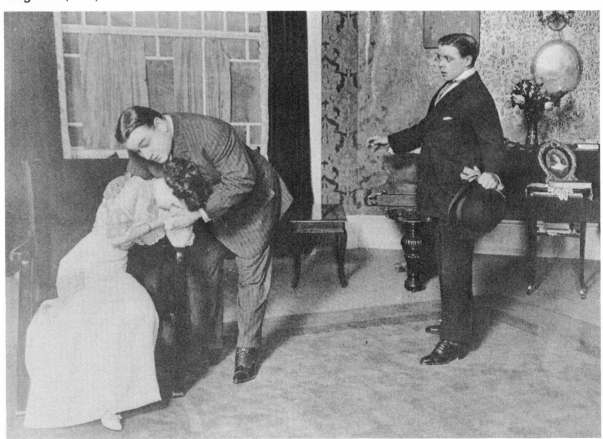

Harold's hat, thrown off in the excitement of the rescue, came sailing into the audience and landing in the lap of a fair lady in the second row of the orchestra.[52]

Then, too, Marguerite Clark's own dignity suffered a brief ruffling on opening night. It occurred, according to the *Review,* when the stage hands at the Lyric were making every effort to handle the heavy and unfamiliar scenery, and meeting with various mishaps. Marguerite, made up as Shakespeare Jarvis, the little son of Jarvis, "the old itinerant showman," "fluttered in and out among the drops and setpieces curiously watching the exciting scene." Presently she felt an arm go around her shoulder, giving her a rough "hug," and then she was forcefully drawn toward the nearest back-stage exit. Next she heard the persuasive voice of one of the stage firemen say:

"You want to be careful, little boy. It's very dangerous on the stage. You might get hurt."

The "diminutive little actress" shook off the protecting arm and drew herself up indignantly.

"Probably you don't know who I am," she said, coolly making the most of every inch of her four feet ten by elevating her chin loftily.

"No—who are you?"

"I'm Miss Clark," was the freezing rejoinder.

"Oh-h-h," gasped the fireman. "I thought you were one of them stage kids."

And he beat a hasty retreat.[53]

Lights O' London illuminated Marguerite's stage career but dimly. The old piece might have been a hit at England's greatest city in the 1880s, but it did little to change dramatic history in New York during 1911.

The limited success of *Lights O' London* perhaps disillusioned Marguerite Clark with the so-called glamour of theatrical life. That disillusionment she carried over into her "Truth to the Stagestruck" written for the *Chicago Record* during this time:

The "glamour" of the theatre is a greatly overestimated institution. The home girl who goes to a party once a month, sees and lives in a greater atmosphere of real glamour than her little sister of the playhouse. Stories about men who send you huge bouquets of American Beauties, candy by the ten pound, and dinner-supper invitations by the hundred, are stories. To be sure, a girl on the stage if she is attractive, does receive attention from men, but not any more than she would if she were not on the stage.

What glamour that may be invested in the name of "actress" is paid for a thousand times over by the sacrifice of the real normal pleasures of life, and by interminable rehearsals in dark, gloomy, theatres and steady relentless hard work. Youth, fresh of face, pays its price too to win a bit of this dubious "glamour" of the stage, and when once the "glamour" is won for a personality, it is analyzed to be absolutely nothing. In the eyes of young boys and silly school girls it may be wonderful, this "glamour," but in the eyes of men and women, real men and women, it amounts to so little![54]

June, 1911, began for Marguerite Clark by her returning to the Suburban Garden in St. Louis for a summer starring engagement. There she repeated her success in *Peter Pan* with a stock company, and then starred with them in *Merely Mary Ann, Little Lord Fauntleroy,* and *When All the World Was Young.* Late that summer, William A. Brady, New York stage producer, signed her to a three-year contract, and she agreed to continue in *Baby Mine* for the Boston, Philadelphia, and San Francisco engagements of that play—after which Brady allegedly agreed to put her at the head of her own company.[55]

The year 1912 brought Marguerite better things at New York's recently built Little Theatre. "My Little Theatre career," she wrote, "began shortly after the closing of *Baby Mine*"—[incidentally followed by the brief run of *Lights O' London*]. Then Marguerite continued:

Doris Keane as "Ben Mark" and
Marguerite Clark as "Shakespeare
Jarvis" in the revival, *Lights O'
London* (1912).

First came "The Affairs of Anatol" in which I represented the raison d' etre *of one of the affairs; and closely following on the heels of this was that very lovely contrast, "Snow White" which I also played in pictures . . . I realized for the first time the difficulties of playing a child's part when the cast is composed of children. In this play, in which the maids-in-waiting and the dwarfs, with whom I constantly play, are real children, some very amusing things happened.*

Although the play was one which appealed to nearly every age from six to sixty, the audience was, for the most part, a very young one, and rarely a week would pass that some child, more familiar with the fairy-tale than others, would not caution me, in a loud voice, not to touch the poisoned apple, or let the old witch in the door; and one little lad nearly upset the scene, when the dwarfs find Snow White apparently dead, by trying to break this shocking news concerning the body under the table as soon as the dwarfs entered the door. And, of course, being only grown-up, it was my duty to remain dead and to hold the scene together at the same time.

To play with children is to have the double task of appealing to the audience and the cast as well, for while a grown-up cast will respond to what may be only a fair interpretation of a child's attitude, a child-cast never will. I try, therefore, always to approach a scene with the mental attitude of a child, to respond impulsively, which is childlike, rather than by studied effect, which is not. And to this end I am continually studying, not only children in all their varying moods, but those who have always best understood them, as well.[56]

Marguerite Clark wrote in retrospect of *The Affairs of Anatol* and *Snow White*, but the *New York Times* reviewed each of the plays, presented by Winthrop Ames, as it was produced, and concluded of the first that "a very smart entertainment is *The Affairs of*

Anatol at the Little Theatre." The paper announced an all-star cast "with John Barrymore, Marguerite Clark, Katherine Emmet, Isabelle Lee, Gail Kane, Doris Keane, and Oswald Yorke" in Arthur Schnitzler's comedy which opened on October 14, 1912. "Note at the outset that the affairs are not of the common order—business, finance, politics," declared the *Times* and further explained:

They are the affairs of the heart, or what passes for it in the peculiarly sensitive organism of this highly bred, idle, rich young man. For to have had such affairs amid such surroundings, Anatol must have been one of the "aristocracy of wealth," if not of brains. A bit of a blackguard, too, this same Anatol— the sort of chap who will kiss and tell and run away. All of which is far from making Anatol dull.

. . . And one may smile at the sight of Anatol— after a succession of affairs in which one lady has usually been sent on her way to make room for the next—himself caught on the hook. This time it is matrimony from which wiggle as he will, he cannot escape.

Then the *New York Times* turned to John Barrymore as Anatol and decided:

Mr. Barrymore plays here with charming variety and plenty of the right sort of humor. The role of Anatol lies comfortably within the lines of his personality and his art . . . But the sketches are really independent of one another, though Anatol and Max figure in most of them.

The *Times* was quite pleased with the first sketch in the *Affairs of Anatol* titled "Ask No Questions" and charmed with Marguerite Clark as Hilda. The paper summarized:

"Ask No Questions" carries a delightful touch of cynicism. Anatol loves little Hilda, and he is sure that she loves him.
But is she ever faithful?

Marguerite Clark played "Snow White" for Little Theatre-goers in the afternoon and one of the five heroines in "The Affairs Of Anatol" in the evening.

Marguerite Clark as Snow White delighted the children who came to see her in the charming dramatization of *Snow White and the Seven Dwarfs* (1912).

Marguerite Clark as Hilda in *The Affairs of Anatol* **(1912).**

He doubts it. So does his friend Max. Now Anatol, it appears, has developed some powers of hypnotism. And it is Max who suggests that he put Hilda to sleep, then ask her the question. Anatol jumps at the idea, and Hilda, when she comes, is nothing loath to having him try his skill on her. When she sleeps, Anatol cannot bring himself to the point of making doubt a certainty. Finally, after listening to Max's gibes, he sends him out of the room. But before Max goes, Anatol says:

"If I am to know the worst, I'll hear it privately. Being hurt is only half as bad as being pitied for it."

"You'll know just the same, because if she's ----- if she has been ----- then you've seen the last of her."

But after Max has retired, Anatol cannot ask the final question. He awakens Hilda, whereupon Max, reentering, assumes that his friend has been reassured. But Max can still be cynical.

"Perhaps you have made a scientific discovery that women tell lies just as well when they are asleep."

The *Times* concluded of the "Ask No Questions" portion of *The Affairs of Anatol*: "To Mr. Barrymore's good acting in this, and the intelligent cooperation of Mr. Oswald Yorke" as Max, "little Miss Marguerite Clark as Hilda adds a piquant charm and not a little delicate art in the moments following the girl's awakening." The *Times* added in finality, "But good taste marks the presentation of Anatol from start to finish, and the settings are charmingly appropriate and beautiful."[57]

Not long after the play opened, Marguerite allegedly dreaded to play the part of Hilda in the first episode of *The Affairs of Anatol* at the Little Theatre. "She liked the part," wrote *The Globe* on December 18, "up until last Thursday night" and enjoyed acting it. "She blames John Barrymore, who plays the part of Anatol, for the change; she says he has been studying hypnotism and that he tried to hypnotize her while as Hilda 'she is supposed to be put into a hypnotic trance by Anatol.'"

He had been doing it at every performance without anything unusual occurring but "on Thursday night" something happened. When Marguerite spoke Hilda's lines, "When you stroke me like that . . . it makes me feel funny all over," she claimed that she really felt a peculiar tingling sensation.

"Instead of just speaking Hilda's lines, I spoke the truth," said Miss Clark. "I relax completely when I sink back in the chair, and the stroking is very restful and soothing.

"That night when Mr. Barrymore said, 'Its so hard to keep awake. Don't try. Why . . . you can't lift your hand,' I found I couldn't. My line is 'No I can't.' I couldn't even speak the line though I had a very clear consciousness that it must be spoken. Mr. Barrymore probably thought I had omitted it on purpose, and after a moment continued with his lines:

"'You are so sleepy . . . so sleepy. Well, then sleep . . . sleep. You can't open your eyes now.' Hilda has nothing to say for a moment, she's relaxed in the chair.

"The next thing Anatol says is 'Hilda, answer me when I ask: What is your name?'

"I found my name on the tip of my tongue instead of Hilda's. I didn't speak it. I didn't speak at all; if I had, I should have uttered my name. Mr. Barrymore repeated the question, and the impulse was so strong to answer with my own name, although I knew perfectly well that I should say 'Hilda' that it made me tingle all over—just as I did when Mr. Barrymore stroked my forehead in hypnotizing Hilda.

"I don't know what might have happened if Mr. Barrymore hadn't given me an impatient shake as he bent over me. My hand fell from the arm of the chair where it had been resting, and then I was all right again.

"That is the first time I've ever been hypnotized, for I really was hypnotized. Either Mr. Barrymore has become a hypnotist through practicing it every night

in 'Anatol,' or I have become very susceptible to suggestion.

"If Mr. Barrymore should hypnotize me again and I shouldn't come from under the influence so soon, just imagine what might happen! Why I might say the most dreadful things right there before a whole theatre of people and not even know what I said."

John Barrymore, according to the *Globe*, denied Marguerite Clark's charge that he had studied hypnotism and declared that it was one of the subjects about which he knew nothing. Still Marguerite avoided the hypnosis scene with Barrymore after a time by taking the part of Mimi, rather than Hilda, when Doris Keane, who had played this role, left the cast to star in another play. This change occurred later in the season when the *Affairs of Anatol* moved to the Maxine Elliott Theatre.[58]

Marguerite starred in *Snow White and the Seven Dwarfs* simultaneously as she played Hilda in *The Affairs of Anatol*. At matinees in the Little Theatre she was Snow White, while in the evenings, Hilda. She charmed the children who flocked to see her. "Imagine," wrote the enthusiastic *Times*,

one of the prettiest fairy tales illustrated by Maxfield Parrish, Boutet de Monvel, or Edmund Dulac, and you will have a faint conception of what this little production is like . . . Of course, Marguerite Clark in the title part has more to do than anyone else and she is charming. Perfectly child-like in appearance, she played as simply as a child and was thoroughly successful in imparting the right sentiment . . . The maids of honor were all real little girls and many of the dwarfs were children too.[59]

The next season Marguerite returned to the New York stage in a farce at the Longacre Theatre titled *Are You a Crook?* The play opened on the evening of Thursday, May 1, 1913. The *New York Times* found "Miss Clark delightful," but that the play "just misses fire" and "what might have been amusing farce is

Marguerite Clark and Elizabeth Nelson in *Are You a Crook?* (1913).

spoiled by too much haste in production."

"For a little while," reviewed the *Times*,

with Miss Marguerite Clark bewitchingly pretty and fetching as a little lady mad about crook plays, and engaging in amateur burglary on her own account, it looked as if the developments might be most amusing . . . But much of what is now introduced in the second and third acts is foreign to the main idea, and in the end it appears as if the author himself had lost faith in his idea and introduced a "moving picture" scheme to forestall possible criticism of the inconsistencies.

Notwithstanding conditions which must have been trying, Miss Clark played last night with a splendid sense of comic values and sureness of touch that gave convincing testimony of what a really clever little artiste she is. She was distinctly better than her role, in which the laughs most frequently were due to manner of doing rather than to the actual content . . . A very pretty first act gave way to one which should prove a model for any one looking for a lesson on how not to furnish a room.[60]

The *New York Times* proved to be correct. *Are You a Crook?* did "miss fire," and after a very brief period, its run was over.

It was during the brief and declining days of *Are You a Crook?* in early May that Marguerite learned of an unusual and unexpected honor — with a publicity angle — that was to come to her from Sarah Bernhardt whose dramatic abilities Marguerite already enthusiastically admired. According to the *New York Telegraph*:

A pretty tribute by the greatest of all actresses to beautiful American womanhood will be paid at the Palace to-morrow, when Madam Sarah Bernhardt will offer for the first time at that theatre her interpretation of "Phedre." The innovation will be none other than the appearance with her of three prominent young actresses, conceded by Madame

Ernest Glendinning as "Pierrot" and Marguerite Clark as "Prunella," in *Prunella* (1913).
(Courtesy The Condé Nast Publications Inc. © 1914 (renewed 1942))

Bernhardt to be among the most beautiful women now appearing upon the American stage. They are Laurette Taylor, Jane Cowl, and Marguerite Clark, all of whom will appear with Madame Bernhardt, wearing the Grecian robes. "Phedre" will be presented by the French actress only at the performances to-morrow and Tuesday.

New York's entertainment world had taken the divine Sarah to their hearts, and earlier that same week a special performance of Buffalo Bill's big show was given at the Madison Square Garden for her, "the performance being identical with that provided by Buffalo Bill for the late Queen Victoria," and Madam Bernhardt declared afterward that "she had never enjoyed anything more in her life."[61]

St. Louis and the Suburban Garden there beckoned to Marguerite Clark, and with the coming of the summer season of 1913, she again returned for the fourth time to head a stock company. Yet this season it was different. The Oppenheimer Brothers, who controlled the Suburban Garden — likely in cohesion with M. S. Bentham, "a natty little vaudeville impresario" who "engaged the dramatic and musical headliners" — changed the name of the Suburban Garden to the Marguerite Clark Theatre for their city's favorite summer star. So Marguerite happily returned to summer stock in St. Louis to begin her brief season with *Baby Mine*, followed by *Snow White* and *Are You a Crook?*. Near the end of June, she yielded to John Barrymore who was to be the next "stock star" for three weeks, opening with *The Fortune Hunter*.[62]

Marguerite Clark returned to New York and to director-producer Winthrop Ames who had succeeded with *The Affairs of Anatol* and *Snow White and the Seven Dwarfs*. He starred her in *Prunella* or *Love in a Dutch Garden* which opened once more at the Little Theatre on October 28, 1913. "Exquisite Fantasy of Rhapsodic Love," praised the *Times* and added "*Prunella* or *Love in a Dutch Garden* is a Beautiful

Scenes from *Prunella* at the Little Theatre. Above, Prunella's aunts (Marie Hudspeth, Cecilia Radcliffe, Winifred Fraser) are unable to keep Prunella (Marguerite Clark) from eloping with Pierrot (Ernest Glendinning). *The Theatre*, December 1913.

Thing, Play and Acting Poetic" and enthused, "Miss Clark's Prunella Is Lovely and Mr. Glendinning's Pierrot a Notable Achievement—Music a Feature."[63]

The fantasy concerns itself with Pierrot's enticement of the guileless Prunella from the sheltered protection of her three spinster aunts, Privacy, Prude, and Prim. From just inside the hedge of the Dutch garden of her aunts, Pierrot draws Prunella from her upstairs room by saying: "Out here waiting for you is a ladder of dreams. Come down and the dream will come true!" And then he tells her that he is going to his "playground, the world" "where the gardens have no hedges, and the roses no thorns, and where all birds fly free. Pierrette, Pierrette, come out of your cage! Come down!" And Prunella, completely charmed by him, answers: "I—I must! For a moment, for a moment only." But the moment extends to three years, and, in which time, he marries Prunella, leaves her, and then seeks vainly and desperately to find her again. He buys the old house with its Dutch garden where Prunella once lived, from her last surviving aunt, hoping that Prunella will return. He draws his friends around him, but they have forgotten Prunella, and when she does revisit the garden, they reject her. Exhausted, she falls senseless in the garden by a statue of Love, and there Pierrot finds her. He exclaims in joy that her heart still beats, and Prunella answers with the last lines of the play:

For thee, only for thee.
  Quick to thy nest,
Thou weary wandering bird, and
  there take rest!
(Pierrot drops his head on to her breast and sobs.)[64]

"Delicate, quaint, fantastic as a dream," wrote the *Times*, and continued, "the dainty and elusive mood of the play is perfectly attained in the acting and setting and emphasized in the beautifully sympathetic music of Joseph Moorat, which is never for a moment at variance with the theme."

Pleased with Marguerite was the *Times* reviewer. "Of Miss Marguerite Clark's fitness for the flowerlike heroine, Prunella, one felt reasonably sure." As to the details of her portrayal, the writer added: "A picture to cause rejoicing, Miss Clark's Prunella, save in the very deepest emotional sense, is a complete embodiment of the role—dainty, alluring, and full of gracious, winning charm." Then he mentioned a passage of Prunella's indicating her "maidenly modesty and reserve" and given very early in the poetic drama:

Not to allow my thoughts to stray
Beyond the duties of each day
Thus only can I hope to be
A type of maidenly modesty.

This "passage of maidenly modesty and reserve with the conveyed suggestion of restlessness and curiosity she plays," wrote the *Times* "with just the right notes of humor and reserve. And she reads the verse admirably. In fact, both she and Mr. Glendinning are singularly free from that tendency to mouthing and intoning so characteristic of modern actors when handling metrical lines." Ernest Glendinning's Pierrot, the critic found to be "a notable achievement." "All in all," concluded the *Times*, "'Prunella' is an exceptionally lovely thing done in an exceptionally competent way."[65]

Marguerite Clark found a special niche in her heart for *Prunella*, and years later recalled it as "That delightful fantasy, played always with more delight than any other role."[66]

Marguerite Clark in 1913.
(American Magazine)

"Surely the stars are images of love."
Bailey, "Festus"

PART II

THE SILENT STAR

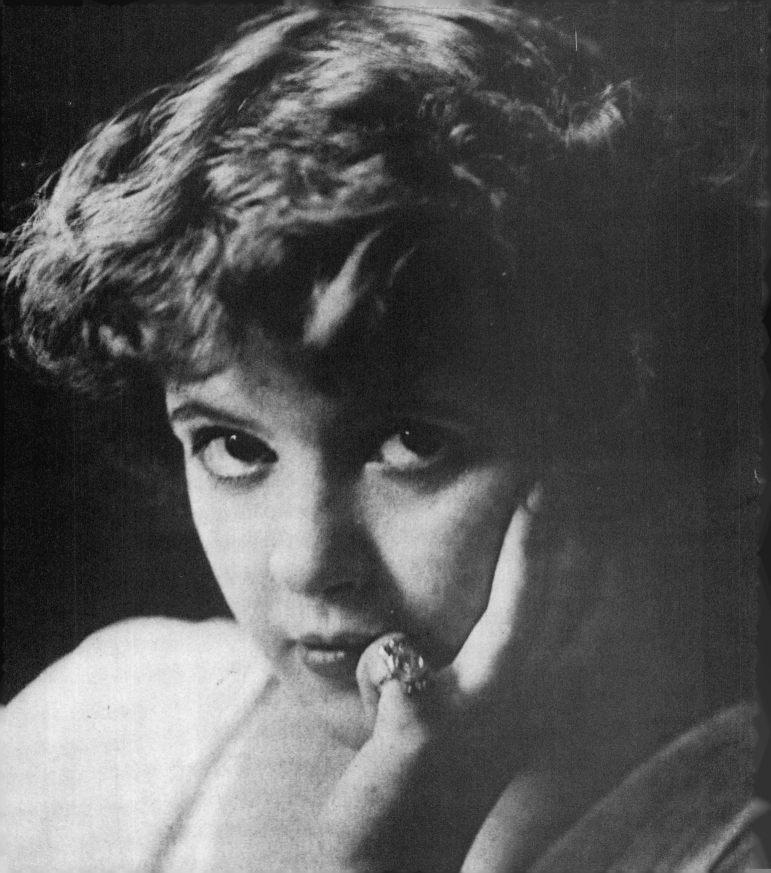

1914 & 1915

 Marguerite Clark found in *Prunella* her favorite stage role, but she also wrote that it was "the direct means of my becoming a motion picture star." To amplify, she added:

Mr. Adolph Zukor was attracted by some photographs of this role and considered offering me a contract to appear exclusively with the Famous Players in the films. He was quite familiar with my work and career, nevertheless, he came to the Little Theatre again and again to assure himself of certain film qualifications. At length, he seemed to think that I would do, and offered me a contract at a salary fifty times as large as I had received for my first work as a star.

Marguerite Clark in 1915. (Buffalo and Erie County Historical Society)

I accepted this most attractive offer, and accordingly decided that, altho I did not wish entirely to forsake the stage or to become identified as a film actress to the exclusion of the spoken drama, I nevertheless would consider for a time appearing only on the screen. For a long time, however, I think I awaited only a suitable vehicle in which to return to the stage but none appeared, and I am still happily associated with the Famous Players and Paramount Pictures, with whom I made my film debut two years ago.[1]

Adolph Zukor, head of Famous Players Film Company, an organization that would soon be a part of the Paramount Pictures corporation, verified that he had been "first struck" with Marguerite upon seeing a photograph of her in *Prunella*. Then he himself went to see her New York appearance in the play *Merely Mary Ann* and was so impressed that he at once took steps to employ her. He sent Daniel Frohman, longtime stage producer, but then working for his company, to attempt winning Marguerite, through Cora, still her manager, into joining Famous Players. Frohman got nowhere with either of the Clark sisters.

Zukor persisted in his efforts to hire Marguerite and told Al Kaufman, his young brother and studio manager, "to stick to the case." Al, a dapper, former barker from Coney Island, did persist, and for seventeen consecutive nights during the run of *Merely Mary Ann* he went backstage and tried to see Marguerite. But Cora—yet a good "stage mother" —barred him at the door. Still, she liked his persistence, and perhaps the thought of the tinkling sound of a great deal of money was appealing too. Anyway, according to Adolph Zukor, a conference was finally arranged between Marguerite, Cora, and him. "I offered one thousand dollars a week." The offer was quite satisfactory as far as the amount was concerned. Yet Marguerite hesitated at signing the three-year contract which he proposed. Zukor wanted to "build her" like Mary Pickford "as strictly a picture star" and not as famous stage actress taking a fling at the screen.

Cora Clark admitted later that she removed Marguerite's hesitation to signing the contract by telling her that "pictures were a fad and in three years would be dead. So she might as well sign."[2]

"It was after 'Prunella,'" Marguerite Clark wrote, "that I made my first picture, 'Wildflower.' Mr. Ames had not been able to find any play suitable for me, to follow "Prunella," so I decided to take advantage of a contract that Daniel Frohman and Mr. Zukor of the Famous Players had offered me.

"That was how I 'broke into pictures.' There was neither effort nor merit on my part. A gold mine was voluntarily offered to me, so to speak. Having nothing better to do, I stretched out my hand and took it. On the part of Mr. Zukor and Mr. Frohman it was a prodigious gamble as nobody had the faintest idea whether *Wildflower* would be a success or an utter failure. Fortunately it was a success thanks to the directors who pushed me through. To this day *Wildflower* is the one of all my pictures that I like best."[3]

Marguerite Clark's performance in her first motion picture, *Wildflower* (1914), was so well received that she immediately became one of the nation's most popular screen actresses.

Adolph Zukor presents

Marguerite Clark

A Paramount Picture

in

"Wildflower"

Story by MARY GERMAINE, Directed by ALLAN DWAN

The public, too, liked *Wildflower*. There was something irresistibly pleasing about the auburn-haired, hazel-eyed actress. The *Theater Magazine* called *Wildflower* "a charming production in every respect." With this first picture, made in 1914, she became a national success and a peer to the extremely popular Mary Pickford. *Wildflower* was only four reels long, and the motion picture cameras used would be considered antique today, but the picture made her famous in a way that none of her stage performances had done. Long after in the 1950s, Joe Franklin wrote of Marguerite Clark and the Paramount picture *Wildflower*:

I think it's interesting that in 1916, a leading fan magazine, Motion Picture Magazine *(and fan magazines had far more substance and influence in those days than they have today) polled its readers to determine their opinions on the greatest screen performances to date. Performances that are still considered great were appropriately appreciated. Walthall's in* The Birth of a Nation *was in third place, those of Mae Marsh and Lillian Gish in the same film were farther down the list. Notable performances by Mary Pickford, Norma Talmadge, William Farnum, and others were duly recorded. Yet Marguerite Clark's performance in* Wildflower—*her first picture—was voted into second place. Since she was beaten only by Earle Williams (for* The Christian*), the indications are that the public at large considered her the screen's finest actress. And at least six other Marguerite Clark's performances placed prominently in the voting!*

So it was that dainty, magnetic Marguerite Clark made her Famous Players debut in pictures. The film, drawn from the novel by Mary Germaine and directed by Allan Dwan, was made in the East with locations not far from the company's studio in New York city. "The action in 'Wildflower' is closely knit," declared one of the advance press stories and continued, "and the pleasing tale is unfolded with ever-increasing interest. Miss Clark makes the character of 'Wildflower' a genuine delight, an elfish, untutored, whimsical little nymph who learns the ways of civilization and who is made the victim of its delicate tortures in the learning." Marguerite Clark was supported by Harold Lockwood as leading man, James Cooley, E. L. Davenport, and Jack Pickford.[4]

Her fame grew with each picture, and before 1914 ended, Marguerite Clark had starred for Famous Players Paramount in *The Crucible*, directed by Edwin S. Porter. Harold Lockwood, then one of the most popular of romantic leads, again acted in that capacity, while Justine Johnstone, a beautiful acquisition from the stage, played a supporting role. In the story filmed like *Wildflower* in New York, a

Above, Jack Pickford, Marguerite Clark, and Harold Lockwood in *Wildflower* (1914).

Below, Harold Lockwood and Marguerite Clark in *The Crucible* (1914).

widow favors an older daughter over a younger one, and unjustly commits the younger girl to a reformatory. The girl escapes, reaches a city, falls in love there, but is kept from being happy by her feeling of unworthiness. The semi-tragic story drew well at the box office, while Harold Lockwood who added much to the plot, proved to be popular with Marguerite.

An executive for Paramount, Samuel Goldfish (later Goldwyn) stated that Harold Lockwood came to him personally during 1915 and tried to bargain for the role of leading man in *The Goose Girl*, Marguerite Clark's next picture, then about to be filmed in Hollywood. But Goldfish disappointed the actor by telling him that Monroe Salisbury had already been signed for the part. Marguerite, too, preferred Lockwood for the role of the male lead, and she definitely did not want to go to California to make the film. Cora held even stronger feelings against going to Hollywood. "What, Marguerite go all the way out to California," she exclaimed to Goldfish, then a partner of Jesse Lasky who was to make the film. Of this incident, Samuel Goldwyn, long after he changed his name from Goldfish, wrote: "An Astor or a Vanderbilt ordered to go out and hoe the potatoes, a Russian nobleman sentenced to Siberia—neither of these could have expressed more profound emotion."[5]

Still Marguerite Clark went to California in 1915 to film *The Goose Girl*, then a popular novel by Harold McGrath, that Jesse Lasky had outbid Adolph Zukor to purchase. Lasky, a one-time vaudeville producer, had but a few years before entered the picture business with a capital of $26,500, creating the Jesse Lasky Feature Play Company. Samuel Goldfish, his brother-in-law, too, joined the organization. Then Cecil B. De Mille entered the company and brought financial stability to it in 1912 through the success of his first directed film, *The Squaw Man*. So Marguerite went to California because Zukor, in the end, agreed that she should go. Lasky asked for the loan of

Marguerite Clark to star in *The Goose Girl*, and Zukor assented. According to Zukor's own words, "The first loan-out of a player, a common thing today, was of Marguerite Clark to Lasky, for *The Goose Girl*. He realized the significance of the precedent—the first major loan by a leading studio of one of its top, contracted stars to another and a rival company.

The loan-out, according to Arthur Marx in his biography, *Goldwyn*, actually began when Samuel Goldfish tried to sign Marguerite Clark at $5,000 a week to star in *The Goose Girl* which Goldfish planned to be his next picture for the Lasky company. He thought the amount would lure Marguerite away from Zukor. But Zukor, this clever, "tiny, ferretlike figure" whom some of his employees called "Creepy" behind his back, outsmarted Goldfish by offering Marguerite $7,000 a week to keep her. Then "to show that there were no hard feelings," loaned Marguerite back to Goldfish for $8,000 a week.[6] Jesse Lasky, head of the Lasky film company, recalled his side of the loan-out and wrote in *I Blow My Own Horn* that when "Marguerite Clark was a magic name at the box office" her contract expired with Famous Players, and he tried to entice her away from the Zukor company "by offering her more money—about $5,000 a week." Zukor then topped Lasky's bid by "a thousand or two and kept her." Then he quite cordially loaned her to Lasky for *The Goose Girl*, which Lasky added "was one of the most successful of our early productions." Lasky said nothing about paying extra for that cordiality. The rivalry between the two companies ended a few seasons later when Famous Players and Lasky amalgamated under the Paramount banner.

Fred Thompson directed *The Goose Girl* which contained sequences of hand-tinted stock and carried a Graustark type of plot that told of a princess of a mythical kingdom who was stolen as an infant and reared by parents who tended geese. A prince fell in love with her and aided the girl in regaining her rightful place on the throne.

The Moving Picture World, a trade magazine for exhibitors, spoke their language in silvered tones and declared concerning Marguerite Clark in *The Goose Girl*: "She conquers her audience in an instant. Petite, dainty, vivacious, gifted, representing a most exquisite type of America's feminine beauty, this little artist takes every heart by storm. . . . When the brave little goose girl is rescued from the clutches of the brutal libertine the whole audience breaks into applause."[7] All in all, *The Goose Girl* turned out to be one of the Lasky Company's most successful productions.

Evident in *Wildflower, The Crucible, The Goose Girl* and most of her other films was a concern for pictorial composition, often delightfully obtained. Some of this, shrewd Cora, as Marguerite's manager, played a hand in, for it was she who approved the directors and cameramen on Marguerite's films. Yet evidently Marguerite herself was a perfectionist. She — not Cora — had aided greatly in making *Prunella* that "jewel box of a play" one of the New York stage critics claimed it to be. Marguerite also lifted the four reel *Wildflower* out of its mediocrity of plot and, through the able hands of Allan Dwan, made it a thing of beauty long remembered after the story was forgotten.

That she valued and accepted Cora's practical suggestions and directions, only indicated Marguerite's own wisdom. Had she rebelled against her intelligent, strong-minded sister — particularly had she done so during those early years on Broadway in musical comedy — there would probably have been no career for Marguerite Clark.

Everybody's Magazine described the California film colony as it was in 1915 when Marguerite Clark was filming the Goose Girl: "It is less than eight years ago that a small organization making travelogues found that Southern California had more varied scenery and

Marguerite Clark in 1915.

At left and right, Monroe Salisbury and Marguerite Clark in *The Goose Girl* (1915). (Eastman House)

Below, *The Goose Girl* (1915) showed the results of Fred Thompson's concern for pictorial composition.

more sunshiny days than any other available spot on the globe. Today Los Angeles is the hub of the photoplay world, the producing center of an industry now rated as fifth in size in the country.

"And the colony is still growing rapidly," the magazine continued. "It is already the Times Square of the theatrical world; more well-known folk from the legitimate stage have summered in and about Los Angeles studios this year than Forty-fourth Street, New York, sees in the winter season." The luminaries named included Nat Goodwin, Billie Burke, Geraldine Farrar, Raymond Hitchcock, Blanche Ring, Carter de Haven, Hazel Dawn, Marie Doro, John Barrymore, Dustin Farnum, Cyril Maude, Marguerite Clark, Flora Zabelle, and many others.[8]

Besides *The Goose Girl*, Marguerite Clark, with little rest in between, zestully completed six more features in 1915 — all of them well done and profitable too for Famous Players. Adolph Zukor did not loan Marguerite out again, and she returned to New York after *The Goose Girl*. The remaining six films made by her in 1915 were: *Gretna Green*, a romantic comedy of eighteenth-century England concerning the wooing of Dolly Erskine, belle of Harrogate, directed by Thomas Heffron, with Wilmuth Merkyl in the lead; *The Pretty Sister of Jose*, filmed too in California and directed by Allan Dwan with Jack Pickford, Rupert Julian, and Edythe Chapman in featured roles; *The Seven Sisters* directed by Sidney Olcott with Conway Tearle as leading man and featuring Madge Evans, a lovely child actress, as the youngest sister; *Helene of the North* directed by J. Searle Dawley with Conway Tearle and Elliott Dexter in featured roles; *Still Waters* directed by J. Searle Dawley, Robert Broderick, Robert Vaughn, and Arthur Evers in the cast; and *The Prince and the Pauper*, Mark Twain's story, directed by Edwin S. Porter and Hugh Ford. William Barrows, William Sorelle, and William Frederick played supporting roles.[9]

Below, Marguerite Clark and Jack Pickford in *The Pretty Sister of Jose* (1915). (Courtesy The Condé Nast Publications Inc. © 1915 (renewed 1943))

The Pretty Sister of Jose was filmed in the mission country of Southern California. Right, Marguerite Clark played the tragic role of "Pepita." (1915).

The Moving Picture World found *The Pretty Sister of Jose* with Marguerite Clark as Pepita, to be a "beautiful picture, perhaps one would not go far wrong in saying the most beautiful picture in which Miss Clark has appeared . . . and offers some uncommonly fine acting." The story, laid in Spain, begins with the death of Pepita's mother, who, no longer beautiful and spurned by her husband, stabs herself with a dagger. Pepita becomes embittered following her mother's death and scorns the love of Sebastiano, a young toreador. Later after Sebastiano has been wounded and is dying, Pepita capitulates at his bedside and admits that she has loved him all along. "Whether the first appeal in *The Pretty Sister of Jose* be attributed to the sympathetic personality of Miss Clark or to the artistic tone and superior quality of the production is of small consequence," concluded the *World* and added that "Jack Pickford is developing as a mature actor in his playing of Jose," and "Rupert Julian makes a forceful Sebastian."[10] Marguerite Clark appeared in only two other films that approached the tragic — *The Crucible* and *Uncle Tom's Cabin*.

She turned to a story of a lighter nature in *Seven Sisters* which was released in August, 1915. "With the always charming Marguerite Clark in the role of Mici, the fourth of seven sisters and a wealth of beautiful scenes to attract the eye, the photoplay adaptation of Edith Ellis Furness' comedy should enjoy a fair measure of popularity"; so predicted the *Moving Picture World*, deciding that "The diminutive star has appeared in stronger stories, but . . . there can be nothing but admiration for the interpretation given the delightfully mischievous Mici." The plot is based on an old Hungarian custom requiring the marriage of the daughters in a family according to their ages. Since her three elder sisters have failed to attract suitors, this is unfortunate for Mici. But, when the older girls pack Mici off to a convent, she escapes

Pictured below, Marguerite Clark (right center) and her leading man, Conway Tearle (far right) in *The Seven Sisters* (1915).

At right, Marguerite Clark as "Mici" in *The Seven Sisters* (1915) a romantic Hungarian comedy.
(Eastman House)

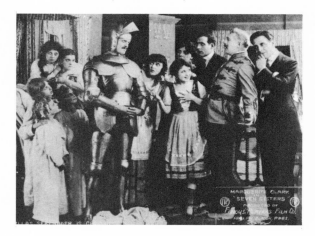

MARGUERITE CLARK
IN
"STILL WATERS"
PRODUCED BY THE
FAMOUS PLAYERS FILM CO.
ADOLPH ZUKOR, PRES.
© 1915

COUNTRY SWEETHEARTS

NESTA JOINS THE CIRCUS

MARGUERITE CLARK
IN
"STILL WATERS"
PRODUCED BY THE
FAMOUS PLAYERS FILM CO.

Above left, country sweethearts in *Still Waters* (1915).

Below left, Marguerite Clark as Nesta became a child of the circus in *Still Waters* (1915).

Below, Robert Broderick and Marguerite Clark in *Still Waters* (1915).

over the wall to attend a masque at which she finds romance in the person of a dashing young lieutenant.

Before the summer was over *Helene of the North* was being shown in theatres all over the country. Again Conway Tearle supported her, and her presence in the role of Helene insured the financial success of the film. In the story, an English woman holds a party at which, once her guests are gathered around the fireplace, they are each given a faggot to burn and required to tell a story while it does so. One of the guests, Helene, tells a tale of romance in the Canadian woods—of the half-breed, Pierre, and his efforts to come between her and Ralph, the young officer whom she loves. The half-breed threatens to kill Ralph if he marries Helene, then seeks to espouse her himself, but the curate whom he has obtained for that purpose, marries her to Ralph instead. At this point, Helene is immediately separated from her new husband, when he is ordered away on "a secret government mission," and she has not seen him since. As fate would have it, however, Helene has no sooner finished with her tale than a new guest is announced at the party: Lord Traverse, who, needless to say, turns out to be the long departed Ralph.[11]

A film critic for the *New York Times* found Marguerite Clark "to be alluring in her girlish and fragile beauty" in *Still Waters,* her next picture where she portrayed "a child of the circus who finally was restored to the grandfather who became estranged with his daughter when she married a circus performer. . . . The grandfather was a canal boat captain, hence the title."[12] The *Times* became more enthusiastic over *The Prince and the Pauper* by Mark Twain, also screened in New York during the fall of 1915 and wrote: "Here is a costume picture that is infinitely superior in every way to the average photo drama. It has thrills and suspense and is full of the romance of the good old swashbuckling days of long swords, long capes, and long hose." The account detailed: "By that trick of the cinema by which one

person may appear simultaneously on the screen in two distinct impersonations, Marguerite Clark is both Prince and Pauper. The effect is accomplished by running the film twice through the camera, exposing one half one time and the other half the next. Miss Clark is altogether delightful in the dual roles."[13]

Marguerite had her problems in enacting the dual roles of these fictional twin sons of Henry VIII of England. Of these experiences she wrote:

I am not even baffled by such instructions as these: "Now you precede yourself into the room; but when you reach the center you look back and see that you haven't come in at all. Then you go back to the entrance, beckon to yourself and come in as before, but engage yourself in conversation. But you don't stand too close to yourself. Remember that you are over at that side door and in the center of the room. Don't come too far down in the center or you will look twice as big as yourself — we must watch the perspective all of the time."

It sounds like the ravings of a maniac. But it isn't. It is simply Hugh Ford telling me how to make a double exposure in such a picture as The Prince and the Pauper.[14]

That year popular magazines noted her success and the *Cosmopolitan* interviewed Marguerite Clark and reported that she said:

"Enjoy being a 'movie' actress? Of course I do, although it really is only play acting. But my own pictures are the best critics of my acting I have ever had. Someone tells you of your faults, but you never pay much real attention to them. But when they are there — the faults, I mean — right before your very eyes — why, there they are! And you can't say, 'Oh, well, I'll be better tomorrow. There isn't any tomorrow. You simply have to do your best today.'

"You think, then, the pictures will help make a good little actress better?"

"One thing I will say," she replied. "You do live the most normal of lives when you are acting in pictures. 'Early to bed, early to rise,' literally. You will run, ride, swim — do, in fact, all the things that make for health and strength."[15]

In the fall of 1915 George Vaux Bacon visited Marguerite Clark for *Photoplay* which featured his story in its March, 1916, issue and carried a painting of her on its cover. His interview, titled "Little Miss Practicality" detailed that:

It was a roasting hot day in early September, and I found her in her pink and white dressing room on the studio floor of the big Famous Players' studio building on West Twenty-sixth Street, New York (which burned to the ground the day after I was there).

Bacon sat on a divan as Marguerite took her place before a big mirror and applied grease paint to her face while they talked.

"Marguerite Clark," he wrote, "is what is termed in the theatre as professionally an 'actress and vocalist.' That is to say she is a singer as well as an actress." Bacon added, "Her eyes are brown, her hair is a reddish brown — almost titian —, she is not married, has no idea of being married, and swears that she was never engaged to be married in her life."

On the subject of romance, Marguerite Clark told Bacon: "I have no desire to have my heart broken, so I always take care not to leave it around or lose it." Later in the interview she admitted: "I am very matter of fact. I know I don't look it, but I am. I am working simply and solely to earn my bread and butter, and my ambition is to find a good play. Do you know of one? No? It is a pity. I shall remain in the pictures until I find one. You see how matter of fact I am. I confess that I really much prefer the stage to the pictures. I know that I am not supposed to say so, but I do. After all, one loves to be able to talk."

Marguerite Clark and Robert
Broderick in *The Prince and the
Pauper* (1915). Double exposure
was used in the film so Miss Clark
could play both the prince and the
pauper. (The Museum of Modern
Art, Film Library)

MARGUERITE CLARK
IN
"THE PRINCE AND THE PAUPER"
PRODUCED BY THE
FAMOUS PLAYERS FILM CO.
ADOLPH ZUKOR, PRES.
C 1915

The Prince proves his identity to Hendon

Marguerite Clark, Wilmuth Merkyl,
Helen Lutrell, and Arthur Hoops in
Gretna Green (1915).

"You are certainly a little Miss Practicality," Bacon told her.

"I am practical, but it's because I've had to be ever since I was a little child. When my sister and I were left, both pretty young, with just a little money in the bank by the death of our father, we decided that we would not touch our capital, but would start out to make some more money so that we would always have a little to add to it. That was how I came to go upon the stage, and we have my first little capital to this day."

Marguerite displayed her practicality on another occasion in a statement she made for stage-struck girls. "So many of them ask me 'how I did it.' I am still doing it and in the same way. Tolstoy tells of a peasant, who while plowing a field, was asked by a priest how he would spend the rest of the day if he knew that he were to die at its close. His answer to the priest is much the same as mine to those who ask how to spend the time between now and success. The peasant answered, 'I would plow.' And this is surely the only way to gain anything worth while and to keep it. I know because I am still plowing."[16]

The New York studio fire mentioned by George Vaux Bacon in his interview, almost completely destroyed Famous Players Paramount. The *New York Times* of September 15, 1915, gave much of its front page to an account of it: "Flames leaped 200 feet into the air and were visible for miles around the city last evening when films, stored in the studio and offices of the Famous Players Film Company in the old Ninth Regiment Armory Building, 213-227 West Twenty-sixth Street, between Seventh and Eighth Avenues, exploded in the midst of a fire which destroyed the building and cost a loss estimated anywhere between $1,500,000 and $3,000,000 and sent firemen and spectators to the corps of doctors from several hospitals overcome by smoke or bruised by heavy streams of water from bursting hose."

The *Times* told of dozens of persons treated by the ambulance surgeons who organized something similar to a field hospital inside the fire lines. The newspaper listed the names of the injured and then told of costly films being lost. "Much of the great loss will be borne by the film company. Adolph Zukor, President of the company, said films worth $150,000 had been stored in steel vaults. . . . Mr. Zukor said some of the films lost were almost priceless." In addition, thousands of dollars worth of costumes burned. "Among the losers in this way," declared the *Times*, "are Mary Pickford, Marguerite Clark, Hazel Dawn, and John Barrymore. Several pets belonging to the actors and actresses, including six canaries, two parrots, and a Persian cat were destroyed."[17]

At the time of the fire, the Famous Players Film Company, a member of Paramount Pictures Corporation, was capitalized at $500,000. Daniel Frohman, long a leading stage producer in New York, filled the position of managing director. Among the well-known actors in the company besides Marguerite Clark, Mary Pickford, Hazel Dawn, and John Barrymore, were Pauline Frederick, Marie Doro, John Mason, and Charles Cherry. These performers had all achieved some degree of success on the stage before turning to motion pictures.[18]

Unbelievably some of the studio's most valuable negatives survived the fire. Throughout the conflagration, a great safe belonging to one of the officials of the company clung to the brick wall of a neighboring structure. Inside the safe were the negatives of two Mary Pickford pictures, a negative of one of John Barrymore's features, negatives of one or more Pauline Frederick pictures and three or four others. Three days after the fire the safe, which had been built to resist heat, was opened, and inside the negatives were found to be almost completely intact —none burned, none melted, and only one "crinkled a little."[19]

The work of the Famous Players company went on uninterrupted. New offices were taken in upper Fifth Avenue, and several studios were placed at the disposal of the company. The pictures announced for exhibition were later shown although in some instances the order of release had to be changed. Some weeks before the fire, the company had announced the purchase of a large tract of land in the upper part of the city as a site for the erection of a large plant, and the fire only hastened the work of its building.[20]

Success marked every foot of film for Marguerite Clark in 1915 and 1916. Everywhere her piquancy was being compared favorably with Mary Pickford, the reigning blonde star of the picture houses. Vachel Lindsay, celebrated poet, declared:

"So let there be recorded here the name of another actress who is always in the intimate-and-friendly mood and adapted to close-up interiors, Marguerite Clark. She is endowed by nature to act, in the same film, the eight-year-old village pet, the irrepressible sixteen-year-old, and finally the shining bride of twenty. But no production in which she acts that has happened to come under my eye has done justice to these possibilities. . . . Her plots have been but sugared nonsense, or swashbuckling ups and downs. She shines in a bevy of girls. She has sometimes been given the bevy."[21]

1916

N o overwhelming offers came to return to the stage, and Marguerite Clark still under contract with Famous Players Paramount continued to make money for the company. There was an indefinable charm about her that lifted what would otherwise have been the most mediocre of films into genuine entertainment. Intelligent, magnetic, experienced by the rigorous training of the musical comedy and the stage, practical yet creative in imagination and genuinely lovely to look upon, Marguerite Clark drew in quite a great number of nickels, dimes, and quarters at the exhibitors' ticket windows all over the nation. "All in all," wrote George Vaux Bacon in *Photoplay*, March, 1916, "she is just a charming,

Marguerite Clark (1916) in a publicity photograph.

fascinating, pretty girl, whose charm is such a strange, wayward, elusively, and delightfully feminine thing that it can no more be set down in words than one can paint humming birds with a sign painter's brush."[22]

It was a day in America when the appearance of innocence and of early youth were both cherished. The ingénue type of actress flourished, and Marguerite Clark and Mary Pickford were adept in such roles. "The movies are best," wrote critic George Jean Nathan of the films of that period, "when they throw aside all posturing and devote themselves very simply to purely sentimental, as opposed to sexual, love. And the drama is quite the worst when it does the same thing." Then he noted the film audiences' preferences for innocence in that day: "The movie public, perhaps not so entirely dumb as many of the Hollywood executives privately like to make it out, has by its patronage long hinted its conviction that sex as Hollywood treats it is silly and has accordingly fallen back for its greater film satisfaction upon the purely sentimental approach. The sex actresses thus come and go, whereas the sentimental ones enjoy an extensive life. The Mary Pickfords and Marguerite Clarks outran in popularity the Theda Baras and Olga Petrovas."[23]

Even the serial queens, such as Pearl White and Ruth Roland, who leaped casually in front of approaching locomotives or who defied hurricanes, tornadoes, and forest fires, never lost their demure girlishness. And though they were chased around many a table by the villains, they were never really winded, and purity did prevail. No wonder this period has been called the Age of Innocence, a time that ended for America with the end of World War I. Certainly it was a day when everybody flocked to the movies.

In 1916, peace still continued in the United States although it was a shaky peace, and Europe had already been involved in war for two years.

Marguerite Clark starred in seven films for Paramount in 1916, and they were titled *Mice and Men, Out of the Drifts, Molly Make Believe, Silks and Satins, Little Lady Eileen, Miss George Washington,* and *Snow White.*

Mice and Men and *Out of the Drifts*, both directed by J. Searle Dawley, received the attention of *Moving Picture World* in early 1916. "It is more than an interesting picture," wrote the *World* of the costumed film *Mice and Men*. "As you walk out from it you feel under its spell. . . . Aside from a few situations, its strength is not in its power, but in its charm." The scenes of the story were laid in the South, and the plot centered around a foundling, Marguerite Clark, who had been adopted in the 1840s by a philosopher with the idea of marrying her if she proved to develop into the sort of girl he had pictured as his ideal. A young male rival, portrayed by Marshall Neilan, caused the philosopher's plan to be changed abruptly. "*Mice and Men* is notable because of Marguerite Clark and that means accomplished and delightful acting. . . . Miss Clark is adorable at all times," thus praised *The Motion Picture News.*

The five reeled *Out of the Drifts* was given bland commendation by the *Moving Picture World* in March. "There are good situations . . . although the subject as a whole depends more upon its average interest than for unusual dramatic quality." Marguerite Clark, in the role of Elsie, a Swiss Alpine maid, who lives alone under the protection of a monk and a guide, falls in love with a young "London sport," (played by William Courtleigh, Jr.), who plans "to lure" her to London with him, but an avalanche intervenes. The young man goes back to England alone only to return in a nobler frame of mind, and marries. Elsie "thereby," snidely reported the *World*, "preventing her 'little' heart from breaking—a bit of titular pathos hardly adult stuff."[24]

Marguerite Clark's films released in 1916 brought favorable newspaper reviews in New York where

Marshall Neilan and Marguerite Clark in *Mice and Men* (1916). A romance of the Old South directed by J. Searle Dawley. (Eastman House)

WHEN YOUTH MEETS YOUTH

MARGUERITE CLARK
IN
"MICE AND MEN"
PRODUCED BY THE
FAMOUS PLAYERS FILM CO.
ADOLPH ZUKOR, PRES.
©1915

legitimate theatergoers still remembered her pleasantly. The *New York Times* reported in April concerning *Molly Make Believe*, directed by J. Searle Dawley, that "Marguerite Clark acted before the lens the role of the little girl who takes her brother and her bulldog to the city to seek their fortune. Molly incorporates herself into a company that furnishes letters to persons ill in mind or body, which eventually brings her romance." The newspaper added that "Miss Clark is one of the most satisfactory of the film stars because in addition to her beauty, which does not suffer in being translated to the screen, she has intelligence. Altogether, *Molly Make Believe* is a picture that will make friends for the movies."[25]

Film followed film in rapid succession—seven, eight a year. In June, the *Times* favored the next of her pictures upon its initial screening and declared: "Marguerite Clark that small and beguiling actress for the screen, who rivals Mary Pickford in popularity, accounted easily for the crowds which flocked to the Strand yesterday for the first showing of her latest picture a mildly romantic photoplay which for no apparent reason is called `Silks and Satins.' " Unimpressed with the plot, the newspaper added: "It tells a tale that might have been filched from the pages of a very old-fashioned novel." The film pictures a modern maiden, moved by the story told in an old diary, that a secret drawer reveals to her, "to obey only the dictates of her own heart in the selection of a husband." "It is a delightful role" for Marguerite Clark reported the *Moving Picture World* in June. Vernon Steele has the leading male part, that of Jacques. . . . It is finely staged and costumed. J. Searle Dawley directs."[26]

Two months later, Famous Players-Paramount released to Broadway viewing *Little Lady Eileen* a film in which, according to the *New York Times*, "Dainty and delectable Marguerite Clark, the complete ingénue of the screen, has a photoplay after her

Below, Marguerite Clark played the role of an ambitious and imaginative child in *Molly Make-Believe* (1916). (Eastman House)

own heart." "Here are Irish dances and colleens and priests—indeed all of the ingredients of an Irish romance as they have it on the stage. And there are fairies to take a leaf out of Irish lore, tiny evanescent, half invisible creatures who dance in an enchanted circle on the green, and at the proper moment, intercede for the downfall of the villain." The *New York Times* detailed: "There is at least one reel that is completely captivating. It is the Irish reel that little Eileen and her sweetheart lead to the merry music of the fiddles. This is a photoplay that is much above the average."[27] J. Searle Dawley directed *Little Lady Eileen* and Vernon Steele played the male lead.

The *Times* liked a farce first shown in New York on November 19, 1916, even better. It stated: "Marguerite Clark, one of the Big Four of movie stars, the other three being Mary Pickford, Douglas Fairbanks, and Charlie Chaplin, was seen in a new film called '*Miss George Washington*' at the Strand. '*Miss George Washington*' is a broadly farcical photoplay. Its plot is spun around a situation that has done service in farces in all languages for all generations and yet there are enough fresh twists to the story and enough charm contributed by Miss Clark and her unusually efficient supporting company to make the picture attractive."

Marguerite Clark's role was that of a mischievous boarding school girl whose reputation for veracity had no basis in fact. A chain of circumstances places the girl and one of her feminine companions in the room of a strange young man in the hotel. Before they can extricate themselves from this predicament they run directly into the father and mother of the other girl. In the panic of the moment, Miss George Washington introduces the stranger as her husband. "The author and director," continued the *Times*, "draw much amusement from a subsequent situation in which the young man and the girl find themselves members of the same house party." The newspaper added: "Forced exhibitions of affection, the

Below, Marguerite Clark as "Felicité" in *Silks and Satins* (1916). "A delightful role for Miss Clark," wrote *The Moving Picture World.* (Eastman House)

preparation of the bridal suite, the interest of all hands in the bride and groom, the increasing terror of the pair as the evening wears on, and finally the efforts of the others to reconcile the pair — these are some of the developments through which the merriment is extracted from the misunderstanding.[28]

Germany's submarines had in May, 1915, killed neutral Americans upon a British merchant liner, the *Lusitania*. No one knew when the Germans would undertake an open, unrestricted submarine war policy on American vessels. Still President Woodrow Wilson sought renomination for the executive office on the slogan "He Kept Us Out of War," and before 1916 was over, he squeeked into a tight reelection over his opponent, Charles Evans Hughes. By the end of December, 1916, war was just around the corner.

Marguerite Clark's motion picture career zoomed toward its zenith. The thirty-three-year-old star — who without let up — had been engaged in theatrical performances since 1899, still looked seventeen — or twelve if she desired. The years of grease paint and dressing rooms of varying quality had left no apparent marks. Any desires for returning to the stage she held, Marguerite Clark controlled, as she went enthusiastically into making one motion picture after another. As to her salary, the *American Magazine* wrote in September, 1916, "Miss Clark gets more than the President of the United States. . . . On Broadway her weekly pay cheque ran close to four figures. Now she not only multiplies her former earnings, but enjoys the luxury of working by the year with no chance of losing her job.[29]

As her popularity grew, she continued to be compared to Mary Pickford. The *American Magazine* found her to be, next to Mary Pickford, the most popular actress in the movies.[30] *Everybody's Magazine* in June, 1916, stated in an article "The Two Most Popular Women in America" that:

Now if the people could vote on a referendum, "Is Mary Pickford the greatest movie-actress, or is

Marguerite Clark?" we should see some voting. We venture to say that the intelligence of the country is several times as well informed on that subject as on "Would Burton make a better President than Borah?" and we are certain that the biggest popuiar movement now extant is the one that is taking millions of people every week to see Marguerite Clark, while those same millions still also go every week to see Mary Pickford; and the two most popular women of American history are running just about reel-and-reel, with Mary Pickford perhaps still ahead by just a film or two.

. . . Both women are young, both are small, both have an appalling capacity for "girlish innocence," and both are devoted (by themselves or their managers) to parts in which innocence and virtue and honesty and kindness and self-sacrifice are carried through inflexibly to the sweet end. We call the attention of haughty despisers of movie morals to the fact that nobody gets really very far in the movies playing parts bearing any resemblance to "Zaza," or "Sappho," or "Iris," or "The Second Mrs. Tanqueray."

Mary Pickford's recent film, "The Eternal Grind," is typical. She works in a sweat shop. How poor she is! And how sweaty is that shop! But how bravely she bears it! And with what cheerfulness she cooks her scanty meals in her squalid rooms! Then comes villainy. She looks into his eyes. And really, she is a magnificent actress, and that is the sort of moment when she is at her best. Her face can change from happy innocence to suspicion, to dread, to flaming hate, while still retaining all its innocence and still

Marguerite Clark as "Bernice Somers," an habitual fibber, in the clever farce, *Miss George Washington* (1916). (Museum of Modern Art/Film Stills Archive)

letting you feel that the girl never did, after all, understand really what the man meant, but only understood that somehow it was vile. So when heroism arrives she is there, clean and lovely, and he is a millionaire—an honest, marrying millionaire—who loves her.

For ourselves, we have often thought that one of the truest criticisms of the morals of the movies would be that most of the most successful films are likely to give young girls excessive notions of virtue's rewards.

Marguerite Clark is more "roguish" than Mary Pickford. Male movie-fans less than sixteen years of age are perhaps likely to prefer her, while females of that same age are perhaps likely to prefer her rival. An experienced critic of our acquaintance, a boy of twelve, informs us that in his opinion Miss Clark is more of a "sport." He means it profoundly respectfully. He means that in "Mice and Men," for instance, she can start on a wild romping run across a lawn, in and out among the trees, and make that run a joy that defies all young-ladyish fatigue and all young-ladyish primness. He means that in "Molly Make-Believe" she can wickedly tease and perplex her lover, where Mary Pickford would lean a bit more toward being "appealing."

They say that in the studios, when there is a spare moment, Mary Pickford is likely to play with the child-actors and Marguerite Clark is likely to read a book. For the adults in their audiences, that is perhaps the difference between them. Mary Pickford's art is rather more instinctively discerning. Marguerite Clark's is rather more reasonedly imaginative.

For fear of riots at the polls, this referendum is now closed.[31]

The best of her pictures for the year was *Snow White*. Edward Wagenknecht in his book *The Movies in the Age of Innocence* said of Marguerite Clark: "I think she is most fondly remembered for the two lovely fairy films she gave us for Christmas in 1916 and 1917; 'SnowWhite' and 'The Seven Swans.' The 'Snow White' exteriors, filmed in Georgia, showed moss hanging from the trees, but the picture missed no element of Christmas appeal; at the beginning Santa Claus even came down the chimney."[32] And he added later, "If you have never seen a Marguerite Clark film, it is like having to confess you have never seen a silver birch or a daffodil."

Walt Disney "traced his selection of *Snow White* as his first animated feature directly to the strong impression the silent film made on him." As a youngster in Kansas City he saw the Marguerite Clark version of *Snow White* at a special news-boys' matinee. The film was exhibited in an auditorium with a four-sided screen in the center and the audience grouped in a circle around it. Disney was seated where he could see two of the screens. The projectors were not completely synchronized, and so he had the experience of seeing the film twice, but with the time lapse between screenings reduced to a matter of seconds.[33]

Marguerite Clark made both stage and screen history for her *Snow White*, while Walt Disney's studios received a special Academy Award in 1939 for his *Snow White and the Seven Dwarfs*. Presented by Shirley Temple, it was in the form of a large Oscar and seven little ones—for each of the seven dwarfs.[34] When Walt Disney's *Snow White and the Seven Dwarfs* reached her home city of New Orleans, the still lovely former star, Mrs. Marguerite Clark Williams, viewed the picture with special interest. Yet dainty, with her jaunty little hat and a gardenia corsage, she permitted herself to be photographed holding a molded figure of one of the dwarfs at a theater where the picture was premiered in her honor.

Marguerite Clark (1916) in a
publicity photograph.

But in early 1917, Marguerite Clark enjoyed the success of her own screened *Snow White*. Adults as well as children forgot approaching war clouds long enough to file into the theaters and lose themselves for a time in the beauty of the fairy story. The *New York Times* found *Snow White* to be an attractive movie version of the Grimm Brothers fairy tale in a stage version of which Miss Clark was seen some years ago at the Little Theatre.

Other publications were more enthusiastic. "Marguerite Clark comes into her own in *Snow White*, the Famous Players Paramount release on Christmas Day. 'Snow White' may not have been made for her, but easily it may be said she was made for 'Snow White.' For into the interpretation of this mite of a princess she puts all of the witchery, charm, and suppleness of which she is capable—and that is saying a lot. Into the direction of the subject, J. Searle Dawley has injected what he knows in the way of artistry, of imagery, of dramatic values—and that too is also saying a lot." The *World* also praised the photography: "H. Lyman Broening was the man who stood behind the camera, the man who skillfully transferred to the screen the shadowy counterpart of that artistry and that imagery and that beauty."[35] The picturesque exteriors were photographed in Georgia. The great trees were "bearded with moss and in garments green," the moss being of the deep-hanging Spanish variety. "In this play," noted the *Motion Picture News*, "Miss Clark is charming beyond words to describe. She fits exactly into the role of the

Princess Snow White, and Creighton Hale as Prince Florimund is a likely match for her charm and beauty."

Marguerite Clark had entered enthusiastically into the making of *Snow White*, since the two seasons she had played the part at the Little Theater in New York under the direction of Winthrop Ames were still fresh in her memory. Nor did she forget Winthrop Ames either, and through her efforts he gave the film company the benefit of his knowledge of staging the subject and also loaned the costumes used in the stage presentation.[36] Later Marguerite Clark said of *Snow White* and *The Seven Swans*, which she made almost two years after, that she "loved" making the fairy tales. "They were so beautiful, it was like living in Fairyland to make them."[37]

Marguerite Clark came into her own on film with the recreation of her stage role in *Snow White* (1916). (Eastman House)

137-18

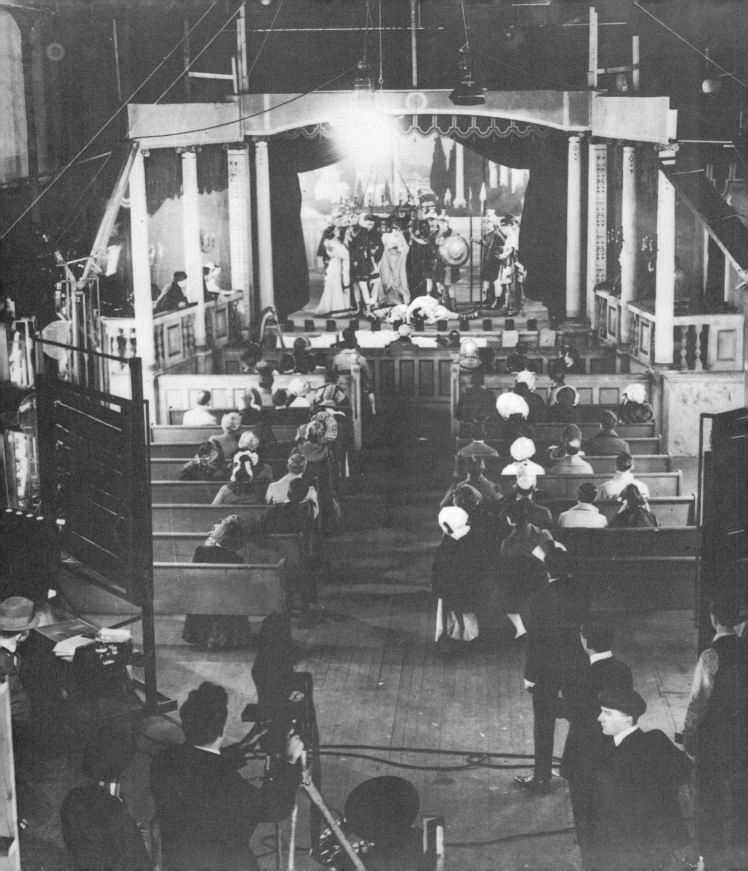

1917

he *Fortunes of Fifi,* directed by Robert G. Vignola, became Marguerite Clark's first picture for 1917, and in the five reel film she played an actress during the days of Napoleon. The photoplay, based on Molly Elliot Sewell's story, had, according to the *Moving Picture World,* "the romantic charm which adds to the zest of life, even when we know things never turn out so beautifully." Still "as Miss Clark plays the part, we are willing to believe in it all." This included Fifi's meeting with Cartouche (a soldier-actor played by William Sorelle); her engagement at the Imperial Theatre; her reception of the gift of a lottery ticket from Cartouche that wins the capital price; the

Fortunes of Fifi (in production).
(Eastman House).

Elsie Lawson, Marguerite Clark,
and Helene Greene in *The Amazons*
(1917).

giving of the award money to the poor in order to escape marrying a man Napoleon had picked out for her; and a happy reunion with her soldier-actor. The reviewer concluded: "The production of the Famous Players Company preserves the quaint air of eighteenth-century Paris with praiseworthy fidelity. . . . The charm given the character by Marguerite Clark is that of perfect innocence and frankness of a child." The *Los Angeles Times* also praised the *Fortunes of Fifi* and called Marguerite Clark a 'piquant sprite.' "[38]

The Valentine Girl appeared in the theaters in late April. Marguerite Clark played Marian, daughter of a professional gambler. The gambler (Frank Losee) turns the little girl over to strangers to rear and then, unfortunately, endures false imprisonment for alleged dishonesty. A youth, acted by Richard Barthelmess, sues for the hand of Marian and eventually wins it, when the good name of her father is restored. "Here is a sure enough good picture. Marguerite Clark as the child of a professional gambler is at her best. She throws into her work all of her charm of impersonation," thus enthused the *Moving Picture World*.

The *Los Angeles Times*, however, was unimpressed and reported: "Marguerite Clark plays the leading role in *The Valentine Girl*, a stock comedy of reminiscent quality, in which the young woman does all the cute things in such case made and provided. It apparently aims at being fanciful—and ends in being as imaginative as a seed catalogue." J. Searle Dawley directed *The Valentine Girl*.

The same newspaper carried an advertisement of the Burbank Theater promising "Any Seat, Any Time a Dime" to see its motion pictures.[39]

That summer she appeared chic and smart in a sophisticated farce titled *The Amazons* that did please the *Los Angeles Times* who wrote: "It took an Englishman—none other than Sir Arthur Pinero—to furnish Marguerite Clark with the most bewitching role she has had in a long, long time. And how this delightful little actress captivates her audiences in the hoydenish character of 'Lord Tommy,' one of the three daughters of an English marchioness, who insists upon bringing them up as boys because she has been bitterly disappointed in her desire for a male heir to the name." Three young men come along at the right time and destroy the plans of the marchioness. Joseph Kaufman directed the *Amazons*, while Elsie Lawson and Helen Greene portrayed the two sisters.[40]

Bab's Diary, directed by J. Searle Dawley, followed closely upon the heels of the *Amazons*. The story by Mary Roberts Rinehart concerned a romantic school girl, home from her vacation and in revolt against the attention shown her debutante sister. In order to draw some attention to herself, she invents a bruised heart and a lover whom she names Harold and then stumbles on to the last name of valentine from a label on a malted milk bottle. She lets letters to him be discovered and feigns loss of appetite to arouse pity. An actor is induced to impersonate "Harold Valentine" just long enough to cure Bab of her deception. Amusing scenes followed, "but the real comedy," according to Louis Reeves Harrison in *Moving Picture World*, "is in a delightful characterization by the author, charmingly interpreted by Miss Clark. . . . Without Mrs. Rinehart's deft and dainty characterization and her sparkling subtitles, the story would be mere froth. Miss Clark, however, exhibits clear comprehension of her role and acts it with high intelligence." Nigel Barrie and Richard Barthelmess both gave able support in *Bab's Diary*.[41] "Miss Clark," wrote the *Motion Picture News*, "fits perfectly into the part of Bab, a seventeen-year-old girl who belongs to the 'flapper' class made famous in recent fiction."

Left and right, Marguerite Clark as "Marian Morgan" in *The Valentine Girl* (1917). *The Moving Picture World* found the film a "sure enough good picture," but the *Los Angeles Times* described it as "as imaginative as a seed catalogue." (Eastman House)

Below, Marguerite Clark
enthusiastically sold Liberty Bonds
during World War I. (Museum of
Modern Art/Film Stills Archives)

In the fall appeared two continuations of the adventures of Bab, *Bab's Burglar* and *Bab's Matinee Idol*, and both films were directed by J. Searle Dawley who took full advantage of the humor of author Mary Roberts Rinehart. Richard Barthelmess was the leading man in these pictures. In *Bab's Burglar*, the sub-deb is given a thousand dollar yearly allowance by her father. The amount is put to her credit in a bank. She buys a runabout, has a minor wreck, and is arrested and fined for speeding. Then she smashes through a fence, backs into a milk wagon, and is fined again in court. All of this in those remote days when a thousand dollars went so far that it covered the entire price of a new car and a series of wrecks. Eventually Bab is left with sixteen cents. Still resourceful, she starts earning money as a cab driver, only to discover what she believes to be a plot to rob her father's house. So Bab lays for the burglar only to catch her elder sister in the act of eloping with a rascal. "'Bab' is a winner," concluded the *Moving Picture World*. The *Motion Picture News* wrote that "Miss Clark has never done anything better."[42]

Bab's Matinee Idol provides a bit of light comedy wherein the persistently romantic Bab is certain she is in love with a matinee idol who hardly knows she exists. The try-out play in which he is featured is a flop, and Bab immediately leads a publicity campaign to save it, but her scheming only results in closing the play sooner than scheduled. The *Theatre Magazine* stated that the Bab stories "make excellent picture material, and with Marguerite Clark as Bab, prove unusually good entertainment. The subtitles are particularly funny."[43]

The "Bab" stories lifted audiences' minds for an hour at least from the events of World War I. Hundreds of thousands of the male youth of the nation were being shipped in war vessels to France, and there they would engage in trench warfare along with their French and British allies against Germany. War taxes were by necessity placed on many things,

Below, Marguerite Clark's feel for comedy was displayed in the picture versions of Mary Roberts Rinehart's Bab stories.

including tickets at the motion picture theaters. Box offices that had charged for children and adults five and ten cents in towns—five and fifteen cents for specials—jumped to ten and twenty-five cents. In cities, the entrance price climbed even more.

War propaganda films continued to appeal, but escapist pictures were exhibited too. Such were Marguerite Clark's films, including the *Seven Swans*, a fairy tale by Hans Christian Andersen which was of the "stuff of which dreams are made." Like *Snow White*, the film was released at Christmas. With Marguerite Clark as a beautiful Princess Tweedledee and handsome Richard Barthelmess as Prince Charming one might possibly forget newspaper headlines and news reels and lose oneself in the beauty of the fairy picture. The film, directed by J. Searle Dawley, was a child's picture, and children flocked to the theater front seats, but older persons came too to be charmed by the *Seven Swans*. *The Moving Picture World* compared *Seven Swans* to Marguerite Clark's *Snow White*. "*Snow White*, Paramount's last season fairy production, has probably been enjoyed by a greater number of persons than any other motion picture ever made. But *Seven Swans* with the same dainty star has been given an even more sumptuous production and forms a most important new chapter in the history of the Land of Make-Believe."[44]

The film industry was stunned by the entrance of the United States in World War I on April 6, 1917. Unrestricted submarine warfare on the part of Germany against the vessels of the United States had caused President Woodrow Wilson to ask Congress to declare war. This declaration followed, and two million American men were eventually sent to France to fight on the western allied front. Young actors left the studios, as youths were doing everywhere, to volunteer for the armed services. Others were drafted. Tom Forman, a well-known Paramount leading man, volunteered and joined the Seventeenth

Company of Coast Artillery, composed almost wholly of motion picture men. Lucian Littlefield, a young character actor, also a volunteer, left for France with the Pasadena Ambulance unit. Wallace Reid, Charles Ray, George Walsh, and Irving Cummings were drafted.[45]

The motion picture industry itself helped in the war effort, for "in teaching war discipline and war organization to citizens the motion picture was remarkably effective. Slides, shorts, and 'picturettes,' featuring popular favorites such as Marguerite Clark, Mabel Normand, and Elsie Ferguson pleaded on behalf of the U.S. Food Administration for 'economy for democracy.' "[46]

The United States Treasury Department asked the motion picture stars to aid in selling Liberty Loan bonds, and Marguerite Clark enthusiastically agreed to give her services when that Department requested her aid in selling them, as their sales, she knew, would provide sums so necessary to finance the war. Marguerite toured the country, making brief patriotic speeches to thousands of potential buyers and adorning floats in numerous wartime parades. Success met her everywhere Marguerite went, and the zealous star sold a total of $18,000,000 in Liberty Loan bonds. Mary Pickford, Douglas Fairbanks, Sr., Charlie Chaplin, Marie Dressler, and William S. Hart were just a few among many notables who boosted such sales by making speeches and cross country tours.[47]

Marguerite Clark raised fifteen million dollars for the Liberty Loan drive at Cincinnati one Tuesday in early November, 1917, when she briefly visited her home town. Marguerite came to Cincinnati at the invitation of Mayor Fuchta and the Chamber of Commerce of the city, "which had designated Tuesday as Marguerite Clark day," and on her arrival she found "awaiting her," said the *Dramatic Mirror*, "a military band, a squadron of mounted police, a company of Home Guards, twenty-five automobiles,

and about 5,000 men, women, and children." Marguerite then received escort to Fountain Square where a Liberty Loan booth had been erected. She mounted the platform and began easily and informally: "My gracious, I can't make a talk, but I am so glad to be here with you. And I want every one to buy a Liberty Bond which our blessed nation is selling."

Bids came quickly, and she raised several hundred thousand dollars within a few minutes, and then Marguerite was escorted to the Chamber of Commerce where she sold more bonds at offices set apart for her use and with her name painted on the door for the occasion. Later, she made further sales at a reception in the ball room of Hotel Sinton and at Fountain Square where she returned briefly.

The city continued to heed her appeal, and "hotel lobbies, meetings, receptions, anywhere in fact that people had gathered were hunting grounds for Miss Clark, and she had secured $920,000 by the time that a big luncheon meeting of the various Liberty Loan Committees was held at the Gibson Hotel."

At the luncheon following the principal speaker, Congressman Nicholas Longworth, Marguerite delivered a "ringing talk" in which she declared that she must have that other $80,000 before she left for New York. Her brief but pointed speech had just been concluded when "Judge Woodmansee, who had been a close friend of Miss Clark's father, the latter having been sponsor for the Judge at the time he was raised in the Masonic Lodge, immediately purchased $5,000 worth of bonds in memory of her old friend." The Judge's purchase introduced further rapid buying, and when Marguerite left after the luncheon, "she knew that she had her million safely secured."

Still millions more were coming, and en route to New York Marguerite received the following wire from J. Maurice Ridge, of the Famous Players Exchange in Cincinnati saying "Gibson Hotel meeting where Miss Clark appeared last raised $14,000,000 which goes to her credit."[48]

Marguerite continued to aid in the war effort in other ways. She knitted in her spare time at the film studio. An interviewer for the *Motion Picture Classic* wrote that during the long waits at rehearsals of *The Amazons* at Famous Players studio in New York, Marguerite kept her hands busy "deftly wielding two long, round implements which, at first glance, looked like a pair of Chinese chop-sticks, but which, upon closer inspection, proved to be a couple of very substantial-looking knitting needles, each over a foot long."

"This is one of my recent hobbies," she said. "When the Comforts Committee Navy League published a request for three definitely approved knitted articles — gray woolen wristlet mittens, sleeveless jackets, and blue woolen mufflers — which if made according to Government specifications could be sent through regular Navy channels to their appropriate destinations, I invested in a set of No. 3 small, amber knitting needles and one hank of gray knitting yarn and attempted to make the simplest knitted comfort, a pair of wristlet mittens, first." Marguerite held them up to view. "Then I bought a set of No. 5 large celluloid needles and three-quarters of a pound of gray knitting yarn to knit this gray worsted, ribbed, sleeveless jacket."[49]

Propaganda feature films flooded the theaters, and among these were *To Hell with the Kaiser, The Kaiser's Finish, Lafayette, We Come, The Woman the Germans Shot* (later changed to *The Cavell Case*), and *The Beast of Berlin*.[50] Marguerite Clark made a feature for Paramount, and titled *Little Miss Hoover* whose name at least struck home to a nation who was everywhere "Hooverizing" on food for the war effort.

D. W. Griffith went to France during the war and filmed *Hearts of the World* close to the battle front. Lillian Gish, Dorothy Gish, and Robert Harron ably starred in this once widely viewed motion picture dealing with life in a French village behind the lines.[51] Griffith began making the picture shortly before the United States entered this conflict.

DURING THE NIGHT SHE KEPT ON WORKING.

MARGUERITE CLARK
" THE SEVEN SWANS"

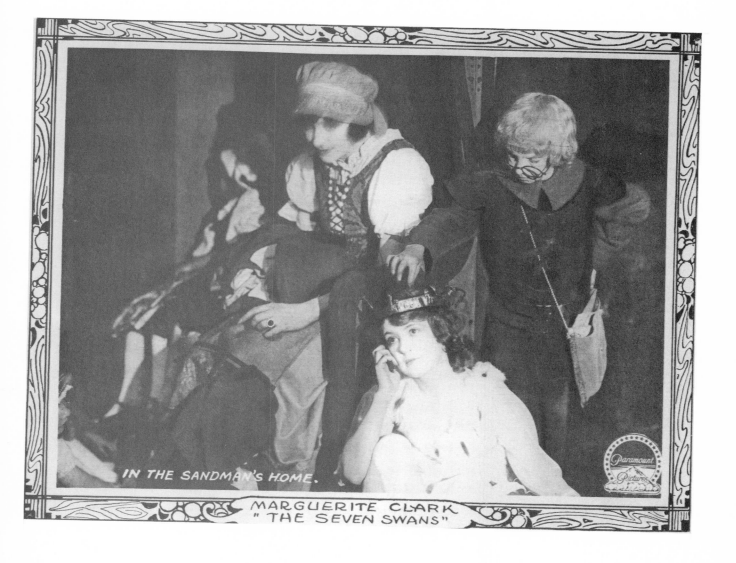

IN THE SANDMAN'S HOME.

MARGUERITE CLARK
" THE SEVEN SWANS"

THE CHANCELLOR GETS A REBUFF.

MARGUERITE CLARK
"THE SEVEN SWANS"

"IS MY CROWN ON STRAIGHT?"

MARGUERITE CLARK
"THE SEVEN SWANS"

1918

By 1918, it was conceded that "screen acting demanded a technique of its own; that stage reputations were of little avail before the camera; that screen stardom had to be earned on the screen."[52] Thus Lewis Jacobs concluded of the time in his *The Rise of the American Film*. Certainly Marguerite Clark had earned stardom of the first rank on the screen, and never once did she depend upon her past stage reputation to aid her.

Intentional or not, rivalry between Mary Pickford and her continued from late 1914 through 1918. Mary Pickford called "America's Sweetheart" and named an honorary colonel during World War I "was at the height of her vogue" and "won the *Motion Picture*

Magazine popularity contest in 1918 with 158,199 votes; Marguerite Clark was the runner up with 138,852." Edward Wagenknecht told of this rivalry in *The Movies in the Age of Innocence* and declared that "it is safe to say that it was Marguerite Clark who gave Miss Pickford most concern, especially during the days when both were with Famous Players."[53] Perhaps Marguerite Clark did not intend to rival Mary Pickford. Certainly Marguerite Clark's first love was the stage not the screen, and she still hoped at some time to return to it permanently. There she had proven herself a celebrity in both musical comedy and dramatic roles. There, too, she had received "critical acclaim from such sophisticates as H. L. Mencken and George Jean Nathan, who for years after she left the stage would recall her unique enchantment." Still it was a time when "the screen was filled with young actresses who, however they might differ" from Mary Pickford and Marguerite Clark "in personality and talent, all cultivated a distinct ingénue line and consciously or unconsciously exerted an appeal of youthful innocence. Among them were Mary Miles Minter, Vivian Martin, June Caprice, Jewel Carmen, and Gladys Leslie."[54]

To Adolph Zukor, the long-time president of Paramount Pictures and once the employer of both Mary Pickford and Marguerite Clark, "Mary Pickford was the first of the great stars." And then he spoke further of actresses of this early period: "We had some fine actresses earlier—Marguerite Clark, Pauline Frederick, Marie Doro, Mabel Normand. Back even farther were Sarah Bernhardt, Lily Langtry, Minnie Maddern Fiske. But all that was a long time ago."[55]

Adolph Zukor wrote too of Marguerite Clark and how her sister, Cora, managed Marguerite's career as did Mrs. Charlotte Pickford, mother of Mary, aid in managing her daughter. The potential rivalry between the two stars he noted as well and stated:

The stage was set for trouble, one might have thought, when I brought in exquisite Marguerite Clark to play roles similar to Mary's. This was particularly true inasmuch as Marguerite's manager and older sister, Cora, was every bit as determined and capable as Mrs. Pickford. . . .

Curiously, Marguerite did not care to be a star. She did not dislike acting. She was merely indifferent to fame.

. . . Marguerite was not lazy, but it was Cora who provided the vast energy and backbreaking work which went into the creation of a star in those days. Cora helped select the plays and coached Marguerite in every detail. I had made a rule that the stars read and answer their fan mail after we had made an analysis of it. Cora searched the letters to discover what the audiences liked best about Marguerite and saw that she answered them.

As to any competition between Marguerite and Mary Pickford, Adolph Zukor admitted that "there was some rivalry between Charlotte and Mary Pickford on the one side and Cora on the other. Marguerite was not interested. But the rivalry was friendly and like that which exists in families."[56] The two remained friends, and years later in 1938, Mary Pickford and her husband, Buddy Rogers, visited Marguerite Clark at her home in New Orleans.

Mary Pickford parted her ways with Paramount, moved to First National, and then on to form United Artists with Douglas Fairbanks, Charlie Chaplin, and D. W. Griffith. Cora took advantage of Mary's departure from Paramount to further Marguerite's interests through suggesting that the tiny star might forsake the screen and return to the footlights. It was alleged that Cora's well placed comments about Marguerite's possibly heeding the call of the stage resulted in Marguerite's becoming one of the highest paid of the stars. Certainly for a time, Marguerite reigned virtually unopposed at the Paramount

studies. Her box office appeal continued to be great, but she was valued at Paramount too for her personal virtues. She was lovely to look at, proficient, cooperative, and best of all—a dependable worker. A true professional, trained to the concept that the "show must go on," Marguerite made reel after reel for Paramount, moving from one feature to another with little time appropriated to herself for rest. "A screen actress," she once wrote, "rises with the rest of the world, works through the world's accepted day, and finishes presumably at its close." And then she continued:

I make on an average eight pictures a year—each followed, if possible, by two weeks rest out of town. But usually many things interfere. There are interviews to be arranged, costumes to consider, plays to read (for I select my own pictures), photographs to sit for—indeed fifty things to do which take all of the time there is.

I receive, like all moving picture actresses, many letters, averaging fifteen hundred a week. I try to read them all, but if I cannot, some one does, and every request for a photograph is fully granted. . . . I live quietly with my sister at Central Park West in the winter and spend the summers at Rye, New York. I never entertain at large parties or appear in public restaurants or places of amusement—I have, as it were, no "Public private life."[57]

Besides Marguerite Clark and Mary Pickford, other prominent actresses of the period were Lillian Gish, Dorothy Gish, Blanche Sweet, Anita Stewart, Alice Joyce, Theda Bara, Mary Miles Minter, Alla Nazimova, Norma Talmadge, Constance Talmadge, Olga Petrova, Beverly Bayne, Pauline Frederick, Florence Turner, Kathlyn Williams, Pearl White, Clara Kimball Young, and Lillian Walker. Leading Actors included Charles Chaplin, Douglas Fairbanks, Wallace Reid, Francis X. Bushman, William Farnum, H. B. Warner, Henry B. Walthall, J. Warren Kerrigan, William S. Hart,

Charles Ray, Tom Mix, Creighton Hale, and Earle Williams.[58] Thomas Meighan, Richard Barthelmess, and Harold Lloyd were all gaining in popularity.

Still with Paramount Pictures, Marguerite Clark reached the peak of her film career in 1918. This was true even though she gave unstintingly of her time in participating in Liberty Bond selling drives and in making short films for the United States Food Administration to aid in the war effort. *Rich Man, Poor Man* was the first picture she made that winter. The film thrived at the box office due to Marguerite Clark's charm rather than to the light plot of George Broadhurst's stage play. *Rich Man, Poor Man* was advertised as "Marguerite Clark's greatest screen success" and provided capable J. Searle Dawley as director and Richard Barthelmess as lead. Others in the cast were Frederick Warde, Geoge Backus, J. W. Herbert, Ottola Nesmith, and Augusta Anderson.

In the story, Marguerite Clark portrayed Betty Wynne, a former boarding school girl, who enters the home of a vindictive financier, Frank Beeston, posing as his grandchild. Beeston is despised by all—except Betty who brought him love and contentment. He learns that she has been foisted upon him but refuses to let her go. Betty eventually finds happiness through the love of a young man who really is the grandson of Beeston.[59]

The next film, *Prunella*, based on the stage play produced by Winthrop Ames both in New York and on the road is remembered as the best of all of Marguerite Clark's motion pictures. Beautifully directed by Maurice Tourneur, the film captured the loveliness of Marguerite Clark, showing her as something exquisite like an orchid blooming uncultivated in tropical wood. It is a tragedy that the film *Prunella* has been lost—that something as delightful as it was only lives in the memories of a few aging devotees of the motion pictures. Perhaps the film would seem dated now, but that is doubtful, as Maurice Tourneur and Marguerite Clark were both

artists. Maurice Tourneur caught for a time on film "her childish face, roguish of eyes and pensive of lips, an oddly contradictory little face, half child's, half woman's, and altogether winsome."

Jules Raucourt made an effective Pierrot, the hero, while other members of the cast were Harry Leoni, Isabel Berwin, Marcia Harris, Nora Cecil, William J. Gross, A. Voorhes Wood, and Charles Hartley. "The play is another product of the artistry of Maurice Tourneur who once more proves his ability to put poetry on the screen in pictures." Thus reviewed the *New York Times* on June 3, 1918, and continued: "Of course many of those who enjoyed *Prunella* at the *Little Theatre* some years ago when Miss Clark first appeared in it, will refuse to accept, silent, flickering figures as in any way adequate to enact the poem, but others, not held by the lingering charm of the play, and still others who did not see the earlier production, will go to the *Strand* this week and be delightfully entertained by Miss Clark." Then the *Times* added in afterthought, "Those who do not like fanciful poetry, costumes, and people of the imagination, will probably be helplessly bored. But that won't be *Prunella*'s fault."[60]

Maurice Tourneur bore within him the touch of greatness. He directed Maurice Maeterlinck's *The Bluebird* contemporaneously and these films Lewis Jacobs, in his *The Rise of the American Film*, found "particularly notable." He declared:

Their subject matter is delicate and philosophic, lacking the conventional situations, and their execution was novel for the screen. Conceived fancifully, they were a fresh and daring escape from the staid realism of the day. Their settings were silhouetted against black drops; costumes were highly decorative; the staging was theatricalized; the whole atmosphere was deliberately artificial. Important though they were as new approaches to film art, however, they had little immediate influence on other American directors.[61]

Upper left, Jules Raucourt as Pierrot and Marguerite Clark as Prunella in the film version of *Prunella* (1918). (Eastman House)

Upper right, Prunella hesitates briefly before eloping with Pierrot, a strolling player. Painted backdrops in poster effect are used here for the first time in motion pictures.

Lower right, Pierrot entices Prunella to leave her home and elope with him.

Some of the settings in the film version of *Prunella* (1918) were silhouetted against black back drops. (Courtesy The Condé Nast Publications Inc. © 1918 (renewed 1946))

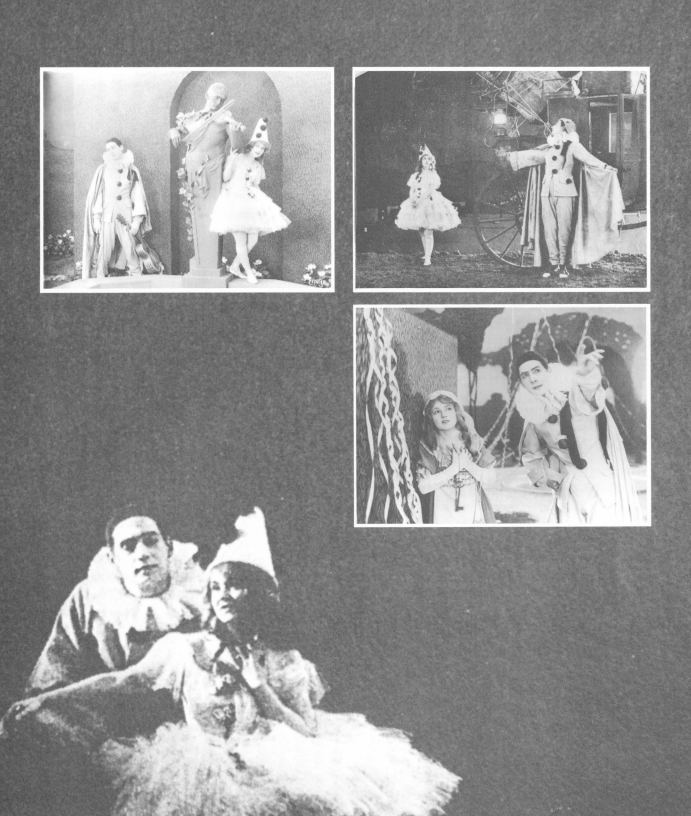

Painted backdrops in poster effect were used for the first time in motion pictures in *Prunella*. Tourneur became acknowledged in 1918 as an outstanding pictorialist of the screen.

There was an "incomparable daintiness and refinement" about Marguerite Clark "which enabled her to outdistance all other stars in whimsy and fairy splendor."[62] These two qualities were most evident in the fantasy *Prunella* which followed so faithfully the stage play.

Prunella proved to be an artistic masterpiece and the greatest of the pictures of Marguerite Clark, yet she was under contract to continue to turn out films for Paramount regularly.[63] There was no time to rest on laurels while she was making, according to *Everybody's Magazine*, approximately seventy-five hundred dollars every week.[64] So shortly after *Prunella* was released, Marguerite Clark entered into the filming of *Uncle Tom's Cabin*. The first showings of the picture hardly crashed upon the nation's attention with the startling effect produced by the appearance of Harriet Beecher Stowe's novel in 1852. Yet the picturization was beautiful, and Marguerite smoothly acted dual roles of Eva and Topsy — although, according to the Los Angeles *Times*, "She was much better as Topsy."

Tragedy occurred in the making of *Uncle Tom's Cabin* when two doubles were drowned at a bad spot in the Mississippi River not far from New Orleans where "there was a swift current and a nasty undertow."[65]

Even Marguerite herself had to brave the Mississippi, according to Frank Losee, the Uncle Tom of the picture, who recalled the incident. "We had troubles too. . . . For instance there was the time Miss Clark and I were immersed. No, it wasn't a christening party, but the scene where she as Little Eva fell into the Mississippi, and it was Uncle Tom's privilege to rescue her. Playing opposite Miss Clark is always an inspiration," continued Losee, "but that scene was positively the most realistic I ever did, because I was actually worried about her; she seemed frightened, altho I knew she could swim."

There was a lighter side to the making of the picture too. One afternoon in the late summer of 1918, the interior scenes of *Uncle Tom's Cabin* were being filmed in the New York studio of Famous Players-Lasky. Frank Losee, his skin darkened for Uncle Tom's part, crouched at the feet of Simon Legree as Legree's great whip curled over Losee's quivering but well padded shoulders. Dorothy Nutting, a writer for *Motion Picture Magazine*, was observing the filming of the scene when she heard a sudden burst of laughter from Marguerite Clark and Director J. Searle Dawley, "both usually determined sticklers for silence during the taking of their scenes."

"Mr. Losee is the funniest man in the world," Marguerite Clark assured Dorothy Nutting. It seems that the bullying Legree had sneered to Uncle Tom that he "owned him body and soul," allegedly following the lines of the book, and Losee had answered solemnly: "No, massa, my soul belongs to God, but my body belongs to — Adolph Zukor."[66]

The film was important to Marguerite for it proved to be the vehicle which drew her, as the picture was made on location near New Orleans, a bit closer to a handsome First Lieutenant Harry Palmerson Williams whose parents' home was in the Louisiana city. At that time, the young officer and plantation owner apparently loved sports, the outdoors, and his home state — but most of all, he seemed to have cared for Marguerite. She returned his affection.

So one could hardly have expected Marguerite Clark, with much of her attention being placed upon affairs of her own heart to have been seriously concerned over heaven bound Little Eva and "just growed" Topsy. Yet, according to the *Moving Picture World*, "Marguerite Clark's double of the little white embodiment of goodness and the small black shadow of mischief is among the most interesting

Marguerite Clark and Frank Losee
in *Uncle Tom's Cabin* (1918).
(Museum of Modern Art Film Library)

of her screen impersonations."[67] The picture was proficiently directed by J. Searle Dawley "with commendable realism," while Frank Losee made an effective Uncle Tom.

Not all of Marguerite's time was given to acting, and she began to spend more of it with First Lieutenant Harry Palmerson Williams of New Orleans. Likable and popular in his home city was Lieutenant Williams, the son of Mr. and Mrs. Frank B. Williams. The personable officer's family held lumbering and sugar plantation lands in Louisiana.

As Adolph Zukor once wrote there was something "exquisite" about Marguerite Clark[68] so it was not surprising that First Lieutenant Williams sought to marry her. And evidently his sincerity, good looks, and enthusiasm all combined to win Marguerite's heart, for on July 26, 1918 she announced her engagement to Harry Palmerson Williams in the *New York Times*. That paper declared:

No date has been set for the wedding of Miss Marguerite Clark, the screen star, and First Lieutenant H. Palmerson Williams, USA, whose engagement has just been announced. Miss Clark arrived here yesterday from Washington, D.C. where she first told of her engagement.

Lieutenant Williams who is also here is attached to the Engineers Corps in Washington. He is the son of Mr. and Mrs. Frank B. Williams of New Orleans, La.

The couple first met while Lieutenant Williams was at school preparing for Yale. Their friendship was renewed when Miss Clark reached New Orleans last winter on a tour to boom the sale of Liberty bonds.[69]

Less than a month later, on August 16, Marguerite Clark and First Lieutenant Williams were married at 11 o'clock in the First Methodist Church at Greenwich, Connecticut, by the Reverend Harley Darley. The *New York Times* reported that "a small group of friends from New York witnessed the ceremony. Miss Cora Clark, who lives with her sister at 50 Central Park

West, acted as maid of honor. The couple later motored to New York."

They were denied a honeymoon trip "for the present as Lieutenant Williams, who is stationed at Washington D.C., has only a brief leave of absence. . . . When they applied for a marriage license from the Town Clerk of Greenwich, both gave their ages at 31. Lieutenant Williams was divorced from his first wife."[70]

(Harry Palmerson Williams' first marriage had taken place in New York City on December 12, 1912, to Marian Hollister, daughter of George Scott Graham, a congressman from Pennsylvania. They were divorced in 1917.)

Nineteen eighteen was a great year for Marguerite Clark. She married the man of her choice; she made *Prunella*, the best film of her career; her War bond sales had been highly successful; and she experienced the thrill of victory when the war itself ended successfully in November.

Out of a Clear Sky and *Little Miss Hoover* were the last two pictures Marguerite Clark made in 1918. Marshall Neilan, a one-time leading man for Mary Pickford, had become, by the war years, an efficient and popular director, and in *Out of a Clear Sky* he turned a quite ordinary plot into a pleasing motion picture. Thomas Meighan, destined to become a star following the splendid *Miracle Man* of 1919 with Lon Chaney and Betty Compson, was Marguerite Clark's very competent leading man. Easy to work with, adaptable, and very likable, Meighan was sought after as lead by many of the feminine stars.

Marguerite Clark announced her engagement to First Lieutenant Harry Palmerson Williams of Louisiana in July 1918. (Museum of Modern Art/Film Stills Archives)

The story of *Out of a Clear Sky* concerned Celeste, a Belgian countess, portrayed by Marguerite Clark, who refuses to become the political pawn of her uncle in his desire to marry her to a German prince. She escapes to America where her uncle follows, but she eludes him by hiding in a secluded area in the mountains of Tennessee. There she gains the aid of Robert Lawrence (Thomas Meighan), a young American who convinces her uncle that she has become the victim of a bolt of lightning. So the old man returns to his political chess, and the countess becomes a Southern housewife in Tennessee. The plot must have appealed to Marguerite Clark who, since her marriage in August, was already contemplating the eventual possibility of giving up motion pictures to become a Southern housewife in Louisiana. The film was released in September, 1918.[71]

Little Miss Hoover, directed by John S. Robertson, was a story about a girl of Washington, D.C., who decides to "do her bit" to win the war by raising chickens. She adopts a slogan "Eggs will win the war," enters zealously into her new endeavor, and meets a young man from the Department of Agriculture with whom she falls in love. This light comedy had Eugene O'Brien as the male lead.[72]

The *Los Angeles Times* voiced mild displeasure over her *Little Miss Hoover*: "Marguerite Clark has a charm—we all admit that. Her managers have discovered this fact, and then insist upon it to the limit. When they put the hard-worked studio scenario writers to pounding out stories palpably made for Miss Clark and nobody else, we feel compelled to rise in protest. For a good work of art is very seldom indeed produced that way. There's neither imagination nor inspiration in the process.

"The photoplay is beautiful, but as a play superficial and insincere, and as a natural consequence, all the actors in it are mechanical, superficial, and insincere. The writer of a play must be honest if he wants to be interpreted by honest actors."[73]

At right, Thomas Meighan and Marguerite Clark in *Out of a Clear Sky* (1918). (Museum of Modern Art/Film Stills Archive)

Below, Marguerite Clark made *Little Miss Hoover* during World War I (1918) when "meatless and wheatless" days were observed in American homes as a part of the "Hooverizing" conservation program. (Eastman House)

1919

 arguerite Clark began 1919 with a salary which out-distanced most of the other film stars. Cora Clark, her clever manager, had seen to that months before Marguerite's marriage. At one of the salary conferences with Adolph Zukor, president of Paramount Pictures, Cora and Marguerite had brought the tiny star's attorney with them, but the lawyer proved a little too glib for Zukor who said to Cora, "Please tell your sister to tell her lawyer to talk more slowly, my mind doesn't work that fast." Yet Cora continued to manage quite well for Marguerite, and when Mary Pickford left Paramount for First National, another film company, and then soon after participated in the forming of United Artists, Cora

arranged for Marguerite "to have the field to herself." Marguerite starred as well at the box office as she did on the screen, but although a winner there, she never topped Mary Pickford. Still she made more pictures per year, and this extra effort lifted Marguerite Clark into the first ten money-making stars of 1918-1919.[74]

Everybody's Magazine wrote a bit enviously in 1919: "It's not many years ago that Marguerite Clark was the pretty tiny foil for large De Wolf Hopper. It is doubtful if her salary ever excelled $300 a week in those days and at very best the theatrical season is but forty-five weeks long. . . . Nowadays she is paid an annual salary of $300,000. All the technical details, all of the cost of production are for other people to worry about. Miss Clark has but to decide upon the plays she wishes produced, dress her parts, and appear before the winking eye."[75]

Marguerite found contentment in the first months of her marriage. Her contract with Paramount kept her busy moving from one film to another, still there was time for home life, and following the end of World War I in November, Harry P. Williams joined her in California.

"Happiness," Marguerite said at this time, "is the most important thing in a woman's life." She continued:

A woman may win success and even a certain amount of fame, but after all, this means very little, and the fulness of her life is best found in a happy marriage. You see, I have thought this all over many times, for I waited quite a while before I married. It seemed to me there were so many unfortunate marriages—one seldom hears of the happy ones—that I felt it safer to drift along as I was than to take the big chance. Though I wasn't particularly happy, neither was I miserable, as were so many whom I knew whose dream castles had fallen.

I had known Mr. Williams for ten years, but we had seen very little of each other for he was either at his home in Louisiana or abroad, and we were just good

friends. Then suddenly, in the face of the war and while awaiting his orders to go across, we discovered it was more than friendship.

We became engaged in May and were quietly married in August. We had to meet the same problem that had come to so many, but there was never a question in my mind that the only thing to do was to be married at once.

Mr. Williams was mustered out soon after the armistice was signed. You know he never got across which broke his heart, but oh, dear, down deep in mine I was glad that we were spared the parting, though I had planned how brave and fine I would be.

After eighteen months in service, he felt he could take a rest, and he is giving this year to me. Every time I go on location or take even a little trip, some one suggests that it is another honeymoon.[76]

Homes became almost a fad to Marguerite at that time, and she insisted on taking an apartment or a house wherever her work brought her rather than moving from one hotel to another. In the first eight months of their marriage, the couple occupied four different houses. The home for her husband and herself during their stay in Los Angeles on Wilshire Boulevard was ready for occupancy on their arrival from New York. "It is a most attractive house," wrote an interviewer, "and while the interior arrangement is elaborate and very beautiful, it has also a homey atmosphere which is very satisfying."

Marguerite Clark's husband, Harry P. Williams, entered as the interview with the actress was in progress. "He is indeed a charming, likeable chap, truly Southern in manner and speech." Maude Cheatham, the interviewer, wrote and added:

Mr. Williams is a great baseball fan and never misses a game. Down in Patterson, La., where the Williams family have their extensive lumber interests, he has a team of his own, and he has discovered several of his former players shining with the coast league. . . .

. . . I soon discovered that her husband does not enjoy sharing his wife with motion pictures and, in fact, he is not very enthusiastic about pictures anyway. He has never been the least of a fan and has seen only a few of Miss Clark's films.[77]

So Marguerite Clark began 1919 with a husband who seemed to have been willing for his bride to continue her career, and certainly he was not discontented with her lucrative contract with Paramount. Yet he was not enthusiastic over her appearing in motion pictures indefinitely, and the fact that her contract was to end in November, 1919, hardly displeased him. "Of course, I wish Marguerite to do as she pleases, and I realize that it may be hard for her to break away from her professional work. She will probably make a picture or two each year, but I confess that I shall not be sorry when she gives it up entirely."[78] Harry P. Williams, according to Jessee Lasky, insisted that there be no scenes made in which his wife kissed her leading man. "This was the kiss of death for Marguerite Clark's popularity." Then Lasky, writing in his *I Blow My Own Horn,* continued, "Every film in those days adhered to the unwritten law of a saccharine clinch at the end. Marguerite's fans expected this as their due and simply couldn't accept their idol as a frigid heroine. Without wasting any time or more dimes at the box-office, they got themselves other idols."[79]

Marguerite certainly lost supporters, but her more ardent and enthusiastic admirers remained loyal, for kisses or not, the star still retained the same grace and beauty. Yet she herself began to contemplate possible retirement, and Marguerite told an interviewer early in 1919 that when her contract did end in the fall of that year, "We will go to New Orleans for the winter," and then, "I do not know what I shall do. I'm not planning. Probably I'll make a picture or two each year, but I shall never make the regular number again."

Then when asked if it would be difficult for her to give up her career, she answered happily, "Not in the least." And she explained, "Oh, of course, it's fine to know that you can stand alone and can amount to something worthwhile by your own efforts, but really I have always been quiet and domestic in my tastes, and then I love New Orleans and the Southern people, and I could be very happy just being Harry's wife and living quietly in New Orleans."[80]

Still in 1919, she went about making motion pictures almost as enthusiastically as she had done when her sister Cora was definitely her manager, and her directors and stories had been scrupulously chosen. Marguerite completed nine films that year, more than she had made in any one of the seven years that she was in motion pictures. These included *Mrs. Wiggs of the Cabbage Patch, Three Men and a Girl, Let's Elope, Come Out of the Kitchen, Girls, Widow by Proxy, Luck in Pawn, A Girl Named Mary,* and *All of a Sudden Peggy.* There was one more she did for Paramount—*Easy to Get*—which was released early in 1920, and this completed her contract with the company.

Mrs. Wiggs of the Cabbage Patch was adapted from the novel by the same name by Alice Hagen Rice, and Hugh Ford directed the film. The picture was released in February, 1919, and the *New York Times* expressed satisfaction with it, stating, "Much of the atmosphere of the comedy and sentiment that made the original so popular has been brought over to the screen. Exceptionally appealing in their roles are Miss Clark as Lovey Mary, Vivia Ogden as Mrs. Hazy, Gareth Hughes as Billy Wiggs and Maud Herford as Mrs. Morgan."[81] May McAvoy played the child, Asia, and Mary Carr portrayed Mrs. Wiggs.

The *Moving Picture World* described *Mrs. Wiggs of the Cabbage Patch* as being "homely, humorous, and heart warming" and found that "Miss Clark as Lovey Mary made the role one enlisting sympathy, but she was so ably supported that honors are widely

At right, Gareth Hughes,
Marguerite Clark, and Vivia Ogden
in *Mrs. Wiggs of the Cabbage Patch*
(1919). (Museum of Modern Art/
Film Stills Archive)

Below, in *Miss Wiggs of the
Cabbage Patch* (1919) Marguerite
portrays "Lovey Mary," a young girl
whose fondness for a child forms
the foundation of the story.

scattered over Mary Carr as Mrs. Wiggs, Vivia Ogden as Tabitha Hazy and others in a line longer than that of the Wiggs children."

As to the story, orphan Lovey Mary runs away from an orphanage taking with her a little boy who has been placed in her care. Mrs. Wiggs, living in poverty with five children, and depending on the Lord to provide, takes the orphans in, provides shelter, and lies for them to a sheriff who seeks to return Lovey Mary and the small boy to the orphanage. Interfering but amusing characters, all friends of Mrs. Wiggs, bring about incidents that improve life for Lovey Mary. She, in turn, proves a godsend, and the whole family attains prosperity.'"[82]

Marshall Nielan directed the five-reel *Three Men and a Girl*, and Eve Unsell made the scenario from Edward Child Carpenter's *The Three Bears*. Richard Barthelmess, Percy Marmont, and Jerome Patrick portrayed the three men, while Marguerite Clark starred as the girl, Sylvia Weston. According to the story, the three men think they hate womankind until they meet the girl. She believes she is willing to marry an animated moneybag who has been selected for her until the time comes for her to say "I do" in the wedding ceremony, when she suddenly exclaims "I do not" and runs away, her bridal veil trailing behind. The three men rent a house on Loon Lake to get away from women. They do not know that the house belongs to the girl, nor has she been informed that it has been rented, and goes there to get away from the man she almost married. A succession of situations follow, and according to the *New York Times*, "all most excellently carried off by the three men and the girl in the cast."[83] Chris Kent, the youngest bachelor, "well played by Richard Barthelmess," falls in love with her, and a reviewer in the *Los Angeles Times* wrote appreciatively, "You can't blame Chris overmuch when you are informed that Sylvia was dowered with all the outward beauties and graces of Marguerite Clark." Yet it was with reservations that the

Marguerite Clark as Sylvia Weston,
the bride who answered, "I do not,"
in *Three Men and a Girl* (1919).

Moving Picture World accepted *Three Men and a Girl* as "little more than a vehicle for dainty Marguerite Clark . . . with only material enough for two or three reels. . . . The personality of Miss Clark helps greatly."[84]

Let's Elope, cleverly directed by John S. Robertson with Frank Mills as leading man, was adapted from Fred Jackson's stage comedy *The Naughty Wife*. The film blithely tells of a young husband who discovers almost too late that he's been neglecting his wife, played by Marguerite Clark, while devoting too much attention to his business. He learns that she's about to elope with his best friend. Yet instead of objecting bitterly, he tries, with pleasantness, to help her carry out the elopement. His unusual attitude causes her to all but leap back into his arms.[85]

In early May, Marguerite Clark's next picture, the pleasing *Come Out of the Kitchen* made its appearance. John S. Robertson again directed. The *New York Times* found him competent and said of this adaptation of Alice Duer Miller's drama of the same name, and of Marguerite Clark's contribution to it, "Another familiar stage play and another favorite of the screen combine to make the multiple reel photo play at the Rialto enjoyable." The newspaper found Marguerite Clark to be "such a cook" as any man "might want to marry, if as the author happily provided, he had sufficient money to hire someone to prepare his meals. She brings out the humorous and romantic possiblities of the character." Marguerite was ably assisted by a cast headed with Eugene O'Brien as the man "with a good eye for cooks." The plot concerns an impoverished but highborn Southern family who pose as servants in their own palatial home when they rent the mansion to Northerners for the summer. They do this in order to provide sufficient money for a costly operation that will save the life of the father of the family. The *Moving Picture World* praised Marguerite, declaring, "Heavy contributor to the joyous mood of this Paramount

At right, Marguerite Clark and Frank Mills in *Let's Elope,* a comedy about a romantic wife and her charming inattentive husband (1919).

Below, Jerome Patrick, Percy Marmont, and Marguerite Clark in *Three Men and a Girl* (1919).

GUERITE CLARK
IN
ET'S ELOPE"

"POOR BOY, HE'S BEEN HERE ALL NIGHT WORRYING ABOUT

comedy is Marguerite Clark, more vivacious, more versatile, more persuasive, than she has ever been, a source of pleasure to the spectator every moment she is on view."[86]

In those early days of her marriage, Marguerite Clark sought to be close to her husband when she made a picture, and no doubt she influenced the production staff of *Come Out of the Kitchen* in their settling on a spot for location not too far from New Orleans. The imposing colonial house chosen for the Southern home of the heroine in the film was at Pass Christian and belonged to a family by the name of Clark—but no relatives of Marguerite. Harry P. Williams would accompany Marguerite on location, and other friends too were allowed to watch the making of the film. One of these guests told years later how Marguerite kept handsome Williams near to her and between takes would kiss him frequently with all the affection of the newly wed.[87]

At right, Marguerite Clark as "Claudia Daingerfield," daughter of a Southern aristocrat, who, due to financial difficulties, becomes a cook in her own home. *Come Out of the Kitchen* (1919). (Museum of Modern Art/Film Stills Archive)

Below, Eugene O'Brien and Marguerite Clark in *Come Out of the Kitchen* (1919). (Museum of Modern Art/Film Stills Archive)

Walter Edwards directed the last six pictures Marguerite Clark made for Paramount. The first of these, *Girls*, was based on Clyde Fitch's stage comedy about three girls who all believe their hearts have been broken by men, and they inscribe on the door of their apartment: "No man shall cross this threshold." But three young men—eligible, pleasing, and persistent—come into their lives, and the sign on the door eventually disappears. "Men are the reason why so many women don't get married," the heroine, Marguerite Clark, states firmly earlier in the film only to relent and become a bride later as do the other two girls. Harrison Ford, with his fine sense for comedy, added much to the film as leading man.[88]

Widow by Proxy, Marguerite Clark's next film, appeared first in New York in September, 1919. In almost all instances the *New York Times* had been kind to her in its reviews through her comic opera, legitimate stage, and motion picture careers, but its film critic gave scant praise to *Widow by Proxy*. The *Times* declared that the film "gives Marguerte Clark an opportunity to be at her cute and kittenish best, and in her way, Miss Clark has pantomime ability. If the picture were not so long drawn out, over so many dull and incongruous scenes, it would be wholly entertaining." The newspaper then turned to the cast. "Miss Clark, aided by Brownie Vernon, Gertrude Norman, Gertrude Clair, Nigel Barrie, Jack Gilbert, and Al W. Filson is able to make it amusing here and there, but unable to keep it from becoming tedious at times." The *Times* wrote of the plot: "There is the spirit of light comedy in the situation in which two prim New England women of immaculate ancestry refuse to accept, but have to encounter, a supposed niece-in-law of just human origin, but the manner in which they become demonstrative with affection for her as soon as she tells them that her godmother is a Duchess, and the effusiveness with which they receive an imitation French modiste posing as the Duchess— of such stuff are movies made at their worst."[89] Jack

Below, Mary Warren and Marguerite Clark in *Girls* (1919), a light comedy based on the stage play by Clyde Fitch, directed by Walter Edwards.

Opposite, at bottom, Harrison Ford
and Marguerite Clark in *Girls*
(1919).

Below, Marguerite Clark, Nigel
Barrie, and Brownie Vernon in
Widow by Proxy (1919). (Museum
of Modern Art/Film Stills Archive)

Gilbert, mentioned in the cast, is the John Gilbert of later fame.

Luck in Pawn was a light comedy in which Marguerite Clark was supported by Charles Meredith as leading man. The film concerns an artist who is tired of the dullness of her day-by-day existence, so she pawns all she has and goes to a fashionable Renaldo Beach where she spends her money in style. Still she uses her time advantageously and meets a young millionaire who falls in love with her.

In Marguerite Clark's next picture, *All of a Sudden Peggy*, Jack Mulhall, a popular leading man, and later himself a star, played the supporting role. Marguerite was charming in the film, and Jack Mulhall, in a note to the author in June of 1978, described her as "the Alpha and Omega of the Theatre."[90]

All of a Sudden Peggy begins with a wealthy British zoologist, a specialist in spiders, inviting a widow to come to his home and aid him in writing a book. The woman arrives with her daughter Peggy — Marguerite Clark. Peggy's mother and the zoologist fall in love. Jimmy, the younger brother of the zoologist appears from London, but Peggy indicates little interest in him. Then when her mother tells her that she will not marry the zoologist until Peggy is safely married, Peggy departs for London. She leaves behind a note stating that she has already married Jimmy. A purse snatcher robs her, and, penniless, she goes to Jimmy's apartment, knowing that Jimmy is still at the zoologist's home in the country. But Jimmy makes a sudden return to his apartment, where he not only finds Peggy but reads in the morning paper that he is married to her. A romance, after further complications, develops.

The *Moving Picture World* said of Marguerite Clark's portrayal of the role that "her interpretation of irresistible Peggy is delightful" and found the film to be a "frolicking comedy with a wealth of wit in the subtitles and a laugh at almost every turn of the

At right, Marguerite Clark and Charles Meredith in *Luck in Pawn* (1919).

Below, on the set of *Luck in Pawn* Marguerite Clark accepts an orchid while her leading man Charles Meredith looks on (1919).

wheel. . . . The cast has been wisely chosen, and includes foremost among its members, Jack Mulhall as an ardent and altogether charming lover."[91]

Marguerite Clark became a blonde for *A Girl Named Mary* and had Wallace McDonald as her leading man. Kathlyn Williams, a handsome serial queen of the very early motion pictures and, by 1919, favorite character actress of drawing room dramas, played a featured role and added to the picture by her presence. The plot centered about a secretary whose employer, a society matron, is looking for her long lost daughter. The secretary learns that she is that daughter and then faces the problem of deciding between the love of her supposed mother and the desire to please the real one.

Easy to Get, released early in 1920, was the last of the six Marguerite Clark films directed by Walter Edwards. Its appearance also marked the completion of her contract with Paramount and the end of her activities with the company. A desire to leave the films had increased since her marriage. She no longer contemplated returning to the stage but desired to retire with her husband to his plantation in southern Louisiana near New Orleans where the land attracted her with its semi-tropical beauty. There had been nothing but work, work, work since she joined Paramount in 1914, and she wanted to rest in a land where the tempo of life was slower. Marguerite left Paramount on a pleasing note, for *Easy to Get* was a clever comedy that presented a bride who loses patience with her husband when he tells her that she was easy to get. She decides to prove him wrong and runs away from home. He then pursues her with an enthusiasm he had never shown before in order to rewin her.[92]

Above, Marguerite Clark became a blond for *A Girl Named Mary* (1919), a romantic drama of a long-lost daughter reunited with her mother.

At left, Lillian Leighton, Orral Humphrey, and Marguerite Clark in *All of a Sudden Peggy* (1919), a frolicking comedy with witty subtitles.

Marguerite Clark reached the peak of her film career with *Prunella* in 1918 where her own genius for fairy splendor had blossomed under the direction of the artist Maurice Tourneur. Yet some of her other films after that time were more successful at the box office than the fantasy of *Prunella* as it was still a reportory play and by its very nature would never have the wide audience appeal of the modern *Come Out of the Kitchen* or the homespun *Mrs. Wiggs of the Cabbage Patch*. Nineteen nineteen was not as great a year professionally for her as had been the season before, but her popularity remained strong, and the men of Princeton named Marguerite that year as their third choice for most popular of all motion picture actresses with Norma Talmadge and Elsie Ferguson being their first and second preferences.[93]

"Home is where the heart is."

Pliny

PART III

HOME TO LOUISIANA

 pon the fulfillment of her contract in November, 1919, Marguerite Clark parted company with Paramount Pictures. Months before, and not long after the wedding ceremony, she had decided to give up her career for marriage. Yet she had held to a contract that called for nine pictures. "She accomplished this remarkable feat of finishing them all in 1919," wrote the New Orleans *Times-Picayune*, "and it was estimated that this one year's earnings probably gave her an all-time record for a stage or screen star."[1]

Her husband held little enthusiasm for her continuing a film career and welcomed the likelihood of her returning with him to Louisiana. Even the Gulf-bordered state itself, with its romantic New Orleans and its lush forests of magnolia and pine must have seemed to beckon. Marguerite was getting older. At

Marguerite Clark, on her return to the screen in 1921. (Museum of Modern Art/Film Stills Archive)

almost thirty-seven, it was difficult to look seventeen or even twenty under klieg lights, facing cameras that demanded complete honesty. Nature had endowed her with an exquisite charm. She was like the first jonquil in spring—or like a Southern redbud tree filled with blooms and radiant in March when everything else was dismal gray.

But very early spring blossoms fall easily to the prey of frost, and Marguerite was determined to avoid yielding publicly to the chill of time. The little jonquil had danced and sung and acted before a pleased public from her teens in 1899 to the beginning of the 1920s—slightly over twenty years. She knew that her day in the sun was almost over; one could play the ingénue only so long. So after the Paramount contract was fulfilled, Marguerite Clark found herself free to enjoy both the wealth and leisure which she had earned. Since she first danced in a chorus in Baltimore at sixteen, there had been nothing but work—and though successful on both stage and screen her labors had been strenuous. Still she did not intend to forsake her career completely, but life in warm and friendly Louisiana with her popular husband seemed to promise happiness. In early 1921, she told Frederick James Smith of *Motion Picture Classic* at her apartment overlooking Central Park in New York:

"Of course, I've missed my work—it had been such a part of my life. We live in a typical old Southern mansion at Patterson, Louisiana, just out of New Orleans. My husband's people before him lived in the same home. It's all comfortable and restful and, oh, so secure feeling. I talk over the dinners with the old colored servants, feed the chickens and just relax. There is languor and restfulness in the very air. That is how my days pass. Then there are social things in New Orleans, quite unlike anything you can find anywhere else in America. Of course, I get restive at times."

"My husband promised to let me do two or three pictures a year. I am going to do that. My next may be a comedy, to be done abroad. It is all indefinite yet. You see, I am too lazy and comfortable to rush anything."[2]

"Is there a possibility of your doing *Peter Pan?*" Smith asked Marguerite in his interview of her. The question aroused Marguerite's interest, for there had been a stock season on the stage at Saint Louis in 1909 when she had starred in *Peter Pan.* And so she answered:

I doubt it, although I would love to play it. If I could do some gorgeous thing like Peter Pan, *I would make it my final picture and definitely retire. I want people to remember me at my best. When I left the stage for pictures I was lucky to be starred in Winthrop Ames' exquisite production of* Prunella *and with that as a final stage effort, I never felt the call back to the footlights. I would rather have folks remember my stage work thru* Prunella. *I wish I could do something equally fine in pictures—and then goodbye.*

Smith reported that Marguerite "actually sighed" as she told him this. He found her to be a "diminutive" person and her husband, Harry P. Williams, who was also present "to be almost as diminutive as his tiny wife." Smith then asked her, "How do you reconcile married life with a career?" Of her reply, which she made while Williams was not present, Smith wrote:

Marguerite Clark in her last film, *Scrambled Wives* (1921), which she produced. (Museum of Modern Art/Film Stills Archive)

"It cannot be done," said Miss Clark . . . "It must always be one thing or the other. Now, my husband is a dear, but he can never understand why night hours are necessary in a studio, or why the lights won't ruin my eyes, or why one has to be at work at a certain hour in the morning. You see, husbands are like that. It is age-old and you cannot change it."

Smith then wanted to know what her opinions were on "husbands and married life," and Marguerite told him: "Well, honestly, I love them both." As to the subject of marriage, she added:

"Gracious, I am no authority . . . You can get by safely if you both know that you must give and take. The only other rule I know is to remember that you are not marrying one person, but a family—and to be just as diplomatic with the family as you are with your husband!"[3]

Yet there were many from the film viewing audiences who remained loyal, who admired Marguerite Clark, and who wanted her to stay with them and continue to charm. Then, too, there were rumors that she "had retired from the screen because her career was fading." So she decided to set up Marguerite Clark Productions, Incorporated, and to star in her own picture.[4]

So after more than a year's absence, Marguerite Clark returned to the screen in *Scrambled Wives*. In New York where the Strand Theaters exhibited the picture at Manhattan and Brooklyn simultaneously in May, 1921, the *New York Times* found the comedy "bright in places, but not substantial enough to fill the five or six reels of film allowed it." As for Marguerite Clark, the newspaper declared, "She has a flapper role in this adaptation of the play by Martha M. Stanley and Adelaide Matthews and has little to do beside being cute. She still has the knack for this, so the part gives her no difficulty." Then the *Times* turned its attention to the director. "Edward H. Griffith directed the production and touched it up here and there, but apparently found the job of enlivening 5,000 or more feet of film beyond his human powers. If he had been allowed to make a two-reel comedy out of his material, the indications are that he would have turned out something delightful."

The story of *Scrambled Wives* begins with the elopement of a school girl with a youth whom she scarcely knows. The father has the marriage annulled and takes his daughter abroad. Two years later the girl, her momentary husband, his more permanent wife, and the hero whom the girl hopes to marry for ever and ever, meet with an assortment of "stock individuals" at a palatial residence on Long Island Sound. Here the scrambling of wives starts.[5]

"After her year's vacation, Marguerite Clark has made an independent production of *Scrambled Wives*, a play written originally for the stage and produced on Broadway by Adolph Klauber. The story is light and amusing but the picture's greatest asset is the star." Thus wrote the *Moving Picture World* and added: "The first half moves slowly in spite of the charming vivacity that was never absent from the star's impersonation of Mary Lucile Smith."[6]

With the picture being mildly successful, she felt relieved from any further obligation to the film world. She could go home to her husband in Patterson at the age of thirty-eight and live in contented retirement. About the age when leaders in other professions were just beginning to achieve success, she was free to retire to Louisiana with its magnolia forests and woodlands of cypress and pine. "I knew enough to go home when the party was over and the guests were gone," she said. Yet she had done well indeed in the seven years she had been on the screen, and several years later, Samuel Goldwyn named her as among the ten greatest motion picture stars along with Greta Garbo, Douglas Fairbanks, Janet Gaynor, Wallace Reid, Norma Shearer, Charlie Chaplin, Mabel Normand, Clara Bow, and Marie Dressler.[7]

After *Scrambled Wives* the party had really ended. By 1921, the year this last film was made, Marguerite was thirty-eight. Still exquisite, and possessing as ever that early spring blossom charm, she could not anticipate playing a very young bride much longer as she had done on the stage in *Baby Mine*—while the days of being seventeen on the screen or depicting children as she had done in *Uncle Tom's Cabin* and the *Prince and the Pauper* were over. Size seemed to have destined the elfin Marguerite to be a perennial ingénue. Of this destiny she had long been conscious and years earlier wrote: "I might long to be as big as Mrs. Siddons and hanker for the gift of tragedy as it is played by Bernhardt and Duse. But there's a place for the little as well as the big in the crowded elevator of life. All we have to do is to squeeze in and wriggle a space for ourselves as we turn to face the door. And if the big ones get the air and the view, well, the little ones, at any rate, don't have to fear that their faces will be scratched by the big one's hat pins." Still she continued to regret being diminutive and added: "It is a distinct disadvantage to an actress to be very small and girlish because that so restricts her as to roles she can fill. She might have the genius of Bernhardt, but it wouldn't enable her to take the parts of full-grown women. Plays have almost to be written for her, or she must stay in the roles of little girls or even little boys, and that does not make her battle an easy one."[8]

Life in Patterson, Louisiana, proved to be a delightful experience to Marguerite. The beauty of the area charmed her. The liveoaks bedecked with Spanish moss guarded the old houses of the little town like bearded sentinels. Spacious houses, some appearing antebellum with their wide front porches, gave beauty to the town. Even the few store buildings, despite their painted advertising signs of relative freshness and their clean show windows, indicated by the able masonry used in their construction that they had been built by a breed of artisans who loved stone work but were no longer in evidence in the nineteen twenties. No storms from the Gulf blowing inland had ever disturbed the limestone strength of these houses of business. Always in these stores there was time to visit between customers and clerks. In fact, time itself seemed to move leisurely in friendly Patterson. There on sea level one's blood pressure dropped comfortably low, and a person could drink barrels of coffee loaded with chickory and still be relaxed.

Yet the town was small, and the fine old homes whose environs extended to the broad, sometimes blue, Atchafalaya River were few and outnumbered by smaller houses which varied in style according to the time in which they were built. Wood prevailed over brick in the construction of these edifices, for Patterson was a lumbering town. Lumber mill employees lived in small wooden cottages built alike.

Patterson, about ninety miles southwest from New Orleans and close to the Gulf, drew fishermen too, and along the cypress bordered banks of the Atchafalaya River, shrimp boats were in evidence.

Being of good family meant much in Patterson just as it did all over the South, and there was no family there and few in New Orleans, more esteemed than Frank B. Williams, his wife, and his children. Frank B. Williams, father of Marguerite's husband, Harry, brought wealth to himself and his state in lumbering, sugar-cane production, and oil development. Frank B. Williams, whose forebears had come to colonial America from England and whose paternal ancestor had fought as a patriot, a medical officer in the American Revolution, pioneered the development of the Patterson area. Late in life he moved to New Orleans where he occupied a mansion on St. Charles Avenue—still one of the show places of the city. Long after, Marguerite Clark sold the magnificent structure at 5120 St. Charles, and a later buyer created a library there—the Latter Memorial Library—in memory of the purchaser's son who had died valiantly

in World War II. The great house now is a part of the public library system of New Orleans.

Some of the Williams family still lived in Patterson when Harry P. Williams brought Marguerite as a bride to live in a large wooden home which once Frank Williams and his family had occupied.

Marguerite Clark Williams was ever tactful and being very fond of Harry, she grew attached to his family too. This affection for them remained genuine, while the outgoing Williams family took the newcomer to their hearts. The people of Patterson too liked Marguerite. Some of the women, in the fashion of an earlier day, called her "Miss Marguerite" and spoke of her husband as "Mr. Harry." She had known both poverty and wealth, and Marguerite understood and appreciated those of small economic means just as well as she did the highly prosperous.

Yet it was Harry P. Williams whom the people of Patterson most valued. Born there, he was their own. They saw him race boats on the Atchafalaya River and tear back and forth over the narrow, tarvia highway to and from New Orleans—at ninety miles an hour in a foreign made car. They openly admired him. Eventually they elected Harry mayor.

Harry P. Williams was never to be just Marguerite Clark's husband in Patterson, New Orleans, or any part of Louisiana. She was Harry's wife—Marguerite Williams instead. Marguerite was sincerely interested in the welfare of the people of Patterson and of others as well. Meigs O. Frost, of New Orleans, wrote of Marguerite's thoughtfulness: "Although few people knew it, she did many private acts of charity and kindness. She never turned down a former pal of the screen or stage. Every year she took six girls and her husband took six boys living in or near Patterson and gave them a college education. He paid for the boys, she paid for the girls." The New York *Mirror* also noted her benefactions. "She is a contributor as well as a steadfast worker in behalf of countless charities . . . A great part of her kind work is among the Negroes of

Louisiana, where welfare has aroused her deepest sympathy . . . One of her especial interests is the education of children and many of those who have received or are now receiving schooling owe this to her."[9]

Marguerite aided aspiring entertainers as well, and because of her efforts, according to Smith Ballew, Adolph Zukor gave the young band leader and singer from Texas a screen test and then a position with Paramount as co-star to Frances Langford. A successful career followed for him in Western pictures during the 1930s. At the time she helped Ballew, Marguerite told him that she had aided only one other actor to get into motion pictures and that was Douglas Fairbanks, Sr.[10]

In picturesque southern Louisiana, Marguerite Clark found contentment. "She had Broadway and Hollywood at her feet, and yet she gave it all up because she truly loved Harry Williams." Frost wrote for the New Orleans *Times-Picayune* and continued: "Despite the fact that she had been the toast of Broadway, she settled down to the quiet country life in Patterson, taking great delight in it. She had a rose garden and she loved it. She had a flock of white Leghorns and a flock of Plymouth Rocks, and she loved them. She often visited the infirmary for workers in the old cypress mill and used to go to the workers' homes." He recalled too a favorite hobby: "She collected perfume from all over the world, though she seldom used it." Her friends knowing

Marguerite Clark Williams soon after making Patterson, Louisiana her home in 1920. (Dept. of Archives and Manuscripts, LSU, Baton Rouge, La.)

of her interest in perfume, favored Marguerite accordingly. "Everyone brings me perfumes," she told Beatrice Washburn in 1925. "I think I must have nearly a thousand bottles. Friends bring me samples from all over the world," and she then exhibited bottles made like tiny lions, crystal bottles from Italy, little flasks like nymphs, vials from Egypt and Persia and Southern France are filled with seductive fragrances."

Frost was pleased, too, with other facets of her character. "She never permitted a risque line in any part she took . . . She hated to see women drink too much and only sipped her drinks. One of the disappointments of her life was not having children."[11]

Marguerite never forgot the old musical comedy days when she literally sang for a living, and occasionally in small groups she would still sing. Certainly Marguerite did not forget the *King of Cadonia*, the comic opera that had lasted so briefly on Broadway back in 1910 but had provided her with a starring role. That musical comedy had contained some catchy songs which she likely could still recall, but the elaborate sets, the pageantry evidenced in the show, she certainly could not have forgotten. Similar pageantry would be recreated in another elaborate setting where Marguerite would reign briefly in New Orleans as she once had done in the *King of Cadonia*.[12]

The time was February 24, 1924, during the Mardi Gras, and the setting the Duke of Alexis Tableau Ball at the Tulane Theater. The handsome theater had been transformed into a resplendant scene of the Imperial Winter Palace for this first Alexis Tableau Ball. "The Russianized costumes were gorgeous and conformed to the effectiveness of gradiose display." Thus described Arthur Burton La Cour and added, "The acting Tzarista of the Mystic Court was Madam Harry P. Williams—the former famed Marguerite Clark whose dazzling regal robe and mantle were

Marguerite Clark Williams as Tzarista of the Mystic Court at the Duke of Alexis Tableau Ball at the Tulane Theatre in New Orleans during the Mardi Gras season of 1924. (Dept. of Archives and Manuscripts, LSU, Baton Rouge, La.)

unrivalled in magnificence. The costumes of the attending matrons were also exquisite." At midnight, specially invited guests went from the Tulane Theater to the Roosevelt Hotel to participate in a "sumptuous supper dance." There any unrecognized Maskers— and some were well disguised in their make-ups— made themselves known.[13] The *Times-Picayune* of New Orleans, years later, recalled Marguerite's apparel at the ball and wrote in September, 1940, that "local dressmakers still say that the costume created for her at that time cost $5,000 and was the most expensive ever worn by a carnival ball queen."[14]

The Grand Duke Alexis Ball of 1924 was one of the outstanding social affairs of the Mardi Gras season. The affair was not created on the spur of the moment, and its birth was inspired by another Mardi Gras social affair presented the year before. In 1923, the Mystic Club had met success in its presentation during the Mardi Gras, and a number of those who had been a part of this "magnificent spectacle" and several "who were on the waiting list of its limited membership" decided that there was a place in New Orleans for another like organization. So the new group—in which Marguerite Clark Williams was active—came into being "to include wives and other married women as queens and ladies in waiting of the court." The Grand Duke Alexis of Russia had been a visitor to New Orleans in 1872, and at that time the royal visitor allegedly "inspired the impromptu arrival of Rex." Thus the Grand Duke became the patron of this new group of masqueraders who named their ball in his honor. The Grand Duke Alexis extravagances took place in Mardi Gras season at New Orleans until 1928.[15]

Marguerite returned to Patterson after the Alexis Tableau Ball to spend her days at the plantation house and its environs just outside the town. "There really isn't anything very picturesque about us. We live a quiet country life like anybody else. I am busy with my flowers and my dogs, flowers grow like

magic in this warm country and I am free to mess in them all I like," she told Beatrice Washburn of *Photoplay* early in 1925 and continued: "Harry's office is near enough for him to come home to lunch and in the evenings we play bridge or Mah Jong or go to the local moving picture house. Although ours is only a small place the films are as good as in the cities." For Marguerite, life moved pleasantly and unhurriedly on the estate with their thirteen dogs, their chicken farm, their flowers, and their lumber mills. She had grown to love her adopted land where palmettos gave the lie to cold weather, and mocking birds spent the brief, brief winters.

Still Marguerite did not spend all of her time in this comfortable home at Patterson. "Harry is so crazy about sports that we do travel about a bit for football and baseball games at different colleges." She then described trips to Tennessee for the fall games at Sewanee and Vanderbilt universities "where they have several adopted students."

Too, there were occasional visits to New Orleans and less occasional journeys to New York to see Cora, but Patterson was home. The restfulness and beauty of the Evangeline country atoned for the time long ago when she had traveled from one shoddy dressing room to another in smoke-filled train coaches with staunch Cora by her side, touring the country in some musical comedy or legitimate play.

The people of Patterson were fond of her too, and it flattered them that a famous screen actress lived there. Harry had grown up in Patterson, and in their minds they doubtless still thought of him as the "speed kid." They sincerely liked him and appeared glad that he owned half of Patterson. His lumber mills provided the principal industry, while Williams' pine and cyprus forests seemed to stretch as far as the horizon.

The estate fronted on the long, main street of Patterson, but according to one account "it backed on the furthermost limits of Louisiana."

Adorned by great trees that fronted it, the large Williams home spread widely with verandas that skirted the house on every side. The building itself possessed twenty-five rooms with a bath room for every bedroom. It was an old house—no colonial mansion with a Parthenon facade—but built with hospitality in mind, for many to enjoy. The verandas were furnished "like rooms with chaise lounges, divans, tea sets, writing tables, books, magazines, and all the other little intimacies of semi-tropic life." Marguerite's own suite was finished in pale green Venetian furniture with rose silk hangings.

The rambling, comfortable home of Harry P. Williams and Marguerite Clark Williams in the heart of the Evangeline country in Patterson, La. *(Photoplay)*

All around the rambling house were sleeping porches, and all about the grounds were flowers—"roses, oleanders, camelias, sweet olive, night blooming jessamine, and crepe myrtle." These Marguerite and her three black gardeners tended with care. The household had its attachments as well which included five motor cars and a staff of black servants with their families. There were two white aides—the chauffeur—for Marguerite did not drive any of her own cars—and her personal maid.

Independently minded hosts at the Williams home then were thirteen hunting dogs, short-haired, black and white and all fun-loving but bearing sad-eyed countenances. They carried such names as Tino, Clip, Zelly, Grandpa, and Bobby and vied for Marguerite's and doubtless Harry's affection with a cynical, linguistic parrot who butchered his broken English with more fragmented French and Spanish.

There were rumors then that there might be an heir to the Williams fortune, but Marguerite herself denied them with a "sad little smile" and said: "I only wish it were true. I would love nothing better, for I adore children. But my husband and I have to make up for it as best we can by helping out other people's children and giving them a start in the world. Perhaps some day we shall adopt one or our own but we have not come to that decision yet."

There was also a report in early 1925 that Marguerite Clark Williams would return to the films as a star in *Peter Pan*. She had starred commendably in Barrie's play on the stage at St. Louis in 1909 when the press there had exuberated its praise. John S. Robertson was being considered by Paramount as the potential director of *Peter Pan* as he had done some very fine things for the company such as *Sentimental Tommy* with Gareth Hughes and May McAvoy and *Dr. Jekyll and Mr. Hyde* with John Barrymore. Robertson considered Gareth Hughes first for the role, but if a boy was not to be used in the part, then according to De Witt Bodeen in *From Hollywood*, Robertson said

that he "rather liked the idea of Marguerite Clark." He had directed her in *Little Miss Hoover, Let's Elope,* and *Come Out of the Kitchen,* and he knew Marguerite's abilities well.

Robertson's remark was repeated to Marguerite who then declared that she doubted she would be considered for the part.

Yet an offer of some sort did come to Marguerite, for Beatrice Washburn declared, "Mrs. Williams admits that she was offered the role of *Peter Pan* which Marilyn Miller is now playing in New York, and she also admits that some day she may return to the screen."

"I don't expect to, but it is possible that I may. When I first left the screen I thought it would be possible for me to do two pictures a year. But I soon found that it could not be done. You cannot run two jobs at once, and Mr. Williams, like any normal husband, is not anxious to have me work again. Still I do keep up my interest in the pictures and am particularly interested in the strides made by historical pictures in the last few years . . . Mary Pickford is and always has been my favorite screen actress and I am a great admirer of Lillian Gish."

Marguerite Clark never again seriously considered returning to the film world. The infant screen was not ready for her back in 1909 when she had taken St. Louis by storm in *Peter Pan*, and sixteen years later, at forty-two, Marguerite was too old to face discerning cameras in the part. Yet she still retained beauty, and Beatrice Washburn noted, "Mrs. Williams has changed very little since those enchanting days of *The Seven Sisters*. She is still tiny and demure and her red brown hair is worn in a single bob just as it has been for the last six years . . . Her eyes are just the color of her hair and she still deserves the tribute of being one of America's best dressed women."[16]

Yet in 1925, Marguerite Clark apparently cared little for being a part of either the stage or screen worlds. Instead, "She admits that she has worked hard,

admits that she is very lucky, that she adores her husband, that she has no regrets for giving up her career and says quite frankly that she is the happiest woman in the world." Marguerite elaborated upon her own contentment and said: "I know it sounds like a platitude to say so but a happy marriage is life's best gift to any woman. A career is necessarily limited. There comes a point when you can go no further and even if you have gone a long way, life is empty without love. But there are no limits to happiness

Marguerite Clark Williams and Harry P. Williams at home in Patterson, La. (1925). *(Photoplay)*

when you are married to the man you love. It develops every year. I don't believe that marriages are made in heaven—not even mine. It takes time and tact and thought to make a happy marriage, just as it does to make a successful career. But in the end it repays you more than the career can ever do."

Marguerite invariably impressed others with her charm, an appeal that was at the same time modest, unassuming, and simple in quality. She was even a trifle reserved as she gratefully expressed her belief that she had been extraordinarily fortunate and that very little of it had been due to her own efforts. "I realize that for some people to have given up their careers would have been impossible," adding, "but, while I was endowed with a real love of the stage, I was also born with a domestic streak—a tendency that makes me like to knit baby blankets and embroider handkerchiefs and fuss with flowers. And I can truthfully say that only my love for my husband would have replaced my love for my work. He has made up for me a thousand times over, anything that I have given up."[17]

Marguerite Clark Williams, although contented in her role as housewife at Patterson, still frequently accompanied Harry to New Orleans. There her number of friends and associates grew, and it was not surprising that she became active in the Mystic Club one of the esteemed social organizations in the city. In the Mystic Club ball at Mardi Gras Season held on the night of February 6, 1932, she participated in its elaborate historical tableaux which carried the title of "Court of King Louis XIV of Fontainebleau." As in the Grand Duke Alexis organization, the ladies in Mystic Club selected for the court were socially prominent matrons—wives of the members. At the ball, Marguerite promenaded with the rest of the court in the grand march and subsequent promenades. "She was exquisite," recalled one of the guests at the ball, "a tiny jewel dressed in an aqua satin costume of the Louis XIV period, her auburn hair elaborately coiffed

in curls and ringlets—graciously smiling to the guests."[18]

Still Harry P. Williams maintained his residence in Patterson, and as his wife, Marguerite concerned herself with affairs there more than with social events in New Orleans. She took great pride in her adventurous mate who loved speed so much and had no time for inaction. He was over six years younger than Marguerite, having been born on October 6, 1889. Yet in appearance and spirit, she was ever the youthful wife.

Harry never seemed to consider any other place than Patterson to be his home even though his wealthy lumberman father, Frank B. Williams, took his wife and Harry's mother, Emily Seyburn Williams, to live in New Orleans. Yet loyalty remained strong within the Frank B. Williams family, and the wealthy father educated his children well. He taught his sons the lumbering business, the management of sugar plantation lands, and cypress milling. He made them familiar with the oil potentialities of southern Louisiana, and he sent them off to approved schools.

Harry P. Williams received his formal education at Lawrenceville Academy at Lawrenceville, New Jersey, and at the University of the South at Sewanee, Tennessee. Upon the completion of his schooling, he immediately embarked upon learning the lumbering business from the ground up. In the process, during 1906, he ran a dredge boat on lumbering operations. Energetically Harry advanced through many successive stages of the industry until he became general manager of general logging operations for the F. B. Williams Cypress Company, Ltd., in southern Louisiana at Plants No. 1 and No. 2. Although the Depression began in 1929 and lasted through the 1930s, Harry P. Williams continued successfully in the management of lumber companies, sugar industries, and oil projects. By 1936, he was director of the following industrial and banking corporations: Williams, Inc.; F. B. Williams Cypress Company, Ltd.;

Williams Lumber Company, Inc.; St. Bernard Cypress Company; the Louisiana Red Cypress Company; Sterling Sugars, Inc.; Franklin and Abbeville Railroad; Commercial Bank and Trust Company; Patterson State Bank; Williams Oil Syndicate; Black Gold Oil Company; Patterson Light and Power Company, and the Louisiana Moss Products Company. Also, he owned and directed the operation of a number of sugar plantations including Maryland, Calumet, and others centering about the cypress swamps.

Harry P. Williams loved flying and fast planes, so the business interest that evidently lay closest to his heart was Wedell-Williams Air Service Corporation which—about fifty years ago—he formed with James R. "Jimmy" Wedell. The two men located their Air Service Corporation just outside Harry's home town of Patterson. Jimmy Wedell, a young, brilliant, barnstorming pilot and Harry P. Williams, a wealthy sportsman, thus formed their aviation firm, and by the early nineteen thirties their airport was considered to be one of the best equipped in the United States, and the Wedell-Williams monoplanes featured numerous engineering innovations— typified by Wedell's speed winner, the "44"—that were manufactured there. The number forty-four meant much to Harry's partner, Jimmy Wedell, who as a "slim, tousled haired young man" in his "44" plane outdistanced in speed James Doolittle's "Gee Bee," thus gaining a world's record for the Louisiana speedster. Harry P. Williams had chosen his partner wisely. It was reliably said in Louisiana that "if it had wings, Jimmy could fix it, fly it, design it, or build it." All of this he did on "a shoestring of technical training and a wealth of natural ability."[19]

On March 29, 1930, pilots Harry P. Williams and Jimmy Wedell, in two of their own designed and built monoplanes constructed at Patterson, astounded New Orleans in a "spectacular race against time Saturday from Patterson to the Menefee airport here." And the *Times-Picayune* added: "The ships are of the type that the Wedell-Williams flying service intends to manufacture at their proposed aircraft factory here. The ships have been tested under flying speed of 200 miles per hour." The planes covered the ninety-mile run between Patterson and New Orleans in twenty-seven minutes. The flight was "a race against time and ended in both planes roaring across the home port abreast." Soon after, as planned, they did begin to manufacture speed craft and built a successful business.

On the day of the race, Marguerite Clark Williams enthusiastically greeted her husband and Wedell when they landed in New Orleans at Menefee. She was quite proud of her Harry.[20]

Still Harry P. Williams held other interests besides business, flying, and his tiny, beautiful wife. These were political ones. It all began in the spring of 1928 when Governor Huey P. Long named him general manager of the state penal plantation at Angola, Louisiana. He had supported the Governor previously, and Long had not forgotten. In his new office, Harry took steps toward reorganizing and putting the prison system there on a sound business basis. Still he needed further legislative appropriations for satisfactory operation and disagreed with Governor Long over an appropriations bill that Harry did not consider adequate. So Harry resigned after having held the office but a few months and returned to private business.[21]

His brief experience in public office doubtless encouraged Harry to seek a higher state position, and in October, 1930, at a dinner in Patterson honoring him for being the town's most distinguished citizen, Williams announced that he would run for governor in the next campaign almost two years away.

Governor Huey P. Long already had his eyes on the United States Senate, but he was still not ready to back Harry P. Williams—although Harry had previously been loyal to him. "I know nothing about it," Long said when told of Harry's political plans. "But

I will not support him. I will not support anyone who announces prematurely in the next twelve months." Harry learned immediately of the Governor's attitude and appeared undeterred: "It's all right with me. I'm not going to be carried around in a cradle."

His plans for a gubernatorial campaign blossomed briefly and withered away after Williams lunched with Long at the Governor's mansion in Baton Rouge on October 26, 1931. The convincing Governor evidently caused Williams to change plans, for Harry announced to the newspapers that he would withdraw because of the press of private business and instead would support Highway Commission Chairman O. K. Allen, the administration's candidate.[22] Harry P. Williams thus departed from being an active participant in politics.

The Wedell-Williams Air Service Corporation continued to grow at Patterson, and regular flight schedules were established between New Orleans and St. Louis and New Orleans and Shreveport, and later between New Orleans, Dallas, and Fort Worth. After the air mail reorganization by the United States government in 1934, the company was awarded a contract for air mail service between New Orleans and Houston. Then Wedell-Williams Air Service was credited with making flying big business with the largest individually owned air service of its time in America.[23]

Marguerite Clark watched with pleasure the growth of this company which meant so much to the wealthy sportsman whom she had married. Contentedly she served as the mistress of their plantation house in Patterson. She attended the baseball games in the town with Harry and encouraged him in his financial support of the team. His speed boats won him prizes, and she liked to ride in them beside him on the Atchafalaya River that bordered Patterson. She loved his planes best, but he would not let her fly one herself. Yet, as Harry's wife she learned to live with adventure. In early August, 1929, she christened the new amphibian Bayou-Teche in the East River, New York. It was a handsome plane made by Jimmy Wedell and Harry P. Williams in their Flying Service Company. A very brief time after the christening, the plane crashed at King's Mountain, North Carolina, and Marguerite, as well as all of the other occupants, miraculously escaped injury.

A gas stoppage line forced the plane down, and the new amphibian was damaged, but none of the six persons in the plane were scratched. Jimmy Wedell "with the skill that had brought him unscatched through nearly 8,000 hours of flying" brought the plane down in a furrowed cotton patch in the early afternoon of August 9. Wedell treated the plane roughly, knocking off one land wheel, breaking both wings' pontoons, and tips of the lower wing. "This superb landing was made possible by the quick action of Harry P. Williams in the central cockpit, who when the first sputter of the roaring motor gave

Speed-loving Harry P. Williams, builder of planes and pioneer creator of air services — a flesh-and-blood hero for Marguerite Clark's own romantic drama.
(Archives and Manuscripts Dept. of the Earl K. Long Library at the University of New Orleans.)

warning that the engine was going to conk out, immediately lowered the retractable landing gear, leaving Wedell with all his faculties free to devote to the landing which was enough to tax every bit of his skill." Marguerite and the other three passengers had been playing cards—but none of the party was even shaken by the forced landing. Almost the entire population of King's Mountain, including the town's physician, had seen the ship falling, and rushed out to the wreck site.[24]

Marguerite enjoyed being the wife of the mayor of Patterson, and his friends there became hers. Yet they both spent much time in New Orleans, and Harry's father, Frank B. Williams, arranged for them to have a suite of rooms in his stately home on St. Charles. Marguerite was fond of her father-in-law, but she tended to visit New Orleans more after his death in order to help alleviate the loneliness of Harry's mother, Emily Seyburn Williams. Thus it was that Marguerite made new friends in New Orleans who would remain loyal to her throughout the years she lived in Louisiana.

Recently recalling that time in New Orleans, Betty Williams, niece of Harry P. Williams, described her aunt-by-marriage, of whom she was fond, as being "bouyant, tiny, very, very feminine, always dressed in excellent style, and beautiful with auburn hair and hazel eyes." Ann Cane Brown, for many years associated with Williams Incorporated, a family company in New Orleans, knew Marguerite Clark Williams well then and only a few months ago remembered, "She looked to be about twenty and was exquisite in dress. She was lovely, petite, and dainty. All of the Williams family loved her." Frank B. Williams, Harry P. Williams' nephew, verified in September 1978 the genuine affection the entire family held for Marguerite. "She had lots of charm," he added, "and so beautiful—such a good dancer too." Others too recalled Marguerite as she was in the early 1930s. Janet W. Yancey remembered at

New Orleans, a few months ago, that "Marguerite advanced easily into being a social leader in New Orleans. She moved beautifully about a room and liked afternoon teas. She was lovely and fun to be with, and there was nothing coquettish about her. She eventually had her hair dyed darker, and this was done so proficiently one would never have known." Marguerite's tiny feet impressed Mrs. Yancey. "They were so small—only size one—and her shoes had to be made to order." Eleanor Bright Richardson said at New Orleans recently that "anything Harry liked, Marguerite agreed to, for she was crazy about him."[25]

In the latter part of each summer, usually in August when the Evangeline country of southern Louisiana drooped before the sun, Marguerite Clark Williams left her home at Patterson to visit Cora in New York. "The New York summer seems cool to her after the South," wrote a New York newspaper staff writer. In 1932, on one of these late summer visits, Marguerite reviewed her past thankfully in a sentence: "I've had a lovely life." Then she spoke of her pleasant home at Patterson, adding, "I wouldn't want to live anywhere else. Life is more gentle in the South."

Yet she sorrowed for the South in that depression year and said of her chosen land, "The South is so poor." Then Marguerite admitted that, having no children of their own, she and her husband, Harry P. Williams, still continued to send numbers of boys and girls through college. "A year ago," she proudly said of Harry, "he had seven in college at once, " while she herself had three girls there.

Her interests centered at Patterson on Harry and his plane building and not upon New York. "At the moment," wrote the *New York World-Telegram*, "she is enthusiastic over three airplanes her husband designed which are participating in the races at Cleveland. She was the first to congratulate James Haizlip and Colonel Roscoe Turner" who did participate successfully. "Her husband, partner in the Wedell-Williams Corporation, will not fly in the race,

she said thankfully. As for little Mrs. Williams, she wouldn't fly for anything."

In 1932, at New York, there were no regrets for remembered glory. "It would have been like staying too long at a party," she said at her sister's apartment at 50 Central Park West. "They had wanted me to come back many times," she said of motion pictures and added, "and when the talkies came in, I had some flattering offers. It was nice of them to ask me. But I think it would be pitiful to go back. I don't want to ever."

The newspaper declared that Marguerite "knows now that she quit the screen at the 'psychological moment.'" But she was not consciously ending her career then in order to preserve a legend at its height. "I knew I couldn't go on with my career and have a happy marriage too," Marguerite said and added: "My husband was very young and too busy with his lumber and sugar interests to run around with me while I went on with the movies. He couldn't stand it either. He didn't want me to swim in a picture for fear I'd drown, or ride a horse for fear I'd fall. He worried all the time. And he was frightfully jealous of the love scenes. Although heaven knows they were very mild ones comparatively. It was simpler to quit than to go on. But I didn't miss it."

At this time, Evelyn Seeley, *New York World-Telegram* staff writer found "wisps of *Prunella*" in Marguerite and continued:

Mrs. Williams is much the same as you remember her. She is as tiny as ever and her steps as light; she has not grown plump and matronly. Her brown hair is bobbed, but falls into soft curls from a demure centre part. Her big liquid brown eyes are sombre in the creamy pallor of an unrouged face. She wore a beige frock that blended with her soft coloring.

There is still a little of "Prunella" and "Little Miss George Washington" and "Come Out of the Kitchen" in Mrs. Marguerite Clark Williams. But no little girl hangover detracts from her seasoned graciousness.[26]

She continued to return each fall to be with Cora in "cool" New York, and in October, 1933, the Amalgamated Broadcasting Company tempted her into making a radio debut over station ABC where she gave readings from *Snow White and the Seven Dwarfs*, the play which she twice made famous—on the stage in 1912 and on the screen in 1917. It was the first time in more than twelve years since she had made any kind of a public appearance.

Marguerite had never been on radio before and according to the New York *Telegraph* "was deadly nervous until the program went on the air . . . then she forgot about everything except the reading which she did in a delightfully natural manner. Her voice came over the ether as though she had been doing nothing but radio work all her life."

The Amalgamated Broadcasting Company attempted to get her to sign for a series of these broadcasts, but Marguerite told a staff writer of the *Telegraph* that it would be impossible for her to consider it. "I am leaving New York next week . . . I am always anxious to get back to the South with my husband. Our life is very simple there, but it is everything we want—flowers, books, a lovely rambling house, acres and acres of ground, charming friends, our dogs and horses, and, of course, Harry's pet hobby, his airplanes. With such a life, how can Hollywood, the stage, radio . . . any of them hold allure for me?"

Then, her consuming interest was in returning to Harry P. Williams and to Louisiana. She had reasons to be proud of her husband. He was a pioneer in plane travel, and already he and his partner Jimmy Wedell were running an air line from New Orleans to San Antonio. Then, too, Harry and Jimmy had just broken the speed record at the Chicago World's Fair on Labor Day when their Wedell-Williams plane reached the speed of 305 miles per hour.

Marguerite openly admired his enthusiasm as an airman and his ability as a pilot, but she evidently

valued him most for his personal consideration of her. Harry would not allow Marguerite to take long trips by plane, preferring to have her on "terra firma" most of the time where he *knew* she would be safe.[27]

Marguerite continued her annual August visits to Cora and to New York, and there in 1935 she was asked by a *New York World-Telegram* staff writer if she intended to make "a comeback."

"Ridiculous," Marguerite laughed. "I always hated the movies, and even the theater has no interest to me now as a player, although I shall never lose my interest as a spectator."

Marguerite Clark returned to public life briefly after Senator Huey P. Long, of Louisiana, announced from New Orleans on July 15, 1935, that she had been named a member of the Motion Picture Censorship Board of Louisiana. According to the *New York Times:* "The appointments," Long said, "were made by Governor O. K. Allen. Besides Marguerite Clark, now Mrs. Harry P. Williams, A. W. Newlin, a former newspaper man, and a lawyer, yet unnamed will compose the board. Its duties, Long said, are to get better movies for New Orleans and to return the vaudeville circuits to the city."[28] Marguerite's husband was a friend of the shrewd and dynamic Senator Huey P. Long. She appreciated Senator Huey P. Long's political abilities, and immediately after her appointment she announced that "she might take the stump in his behalf," depending on whether he was nominated for the presidency and whether "my husband is willing."[29]

Marguerite did not spend all of her time in New York preparing for her Louisiana censorship duties. She liked the theater too well for that. "I am seeing all of the available plays," she told a *World-Telegram* staff writer. "How hungry you get for them when you are out of town!"

Marguerite added that she planned to visit Suffern, New York, and see Helen Hayes in *Caesar and Cleopatra*. "Miss Hayes is a great artist. On the other hand, I don't know that our artists today are any better than they were when I was appearing. But the plays are. The modern viewpoint toward life, the facing and admission of realities has rejuvenated dramatic writing." Yet the old morality of a pre-World War I American yet haunted her activities. "I still can't go to cocktail parties alone," she laughed. "If Harry isn't available, I get some escort to drag me along."[30]

In August Marguerite took a negative attitude toward any campaigning for Huey Long in his presidential aspirations and said: "Ever since Senator Long appointed me to the Louisiana Censorship Board my name has been tied to so many political rumors. I can spike them at once. My husband is the only politician in the family, and as far as me going on the stump for Senator Long if he runs for President, it just isn't so." She made the statement in New York at 50 Central Park West at an apartment Marguerite "rented" from her sister Cora.

In the city she planned to confer with members of the New York State Censorship Board. "You see," she told her interviewer from the *New York World-Telegram*, "when I begin my duties in October I shall have to know what to look for. I don't think the gangster pictures are exactly for children. But on the whole, I think our board will be liberal. We shall be most concerned with those 'for men only things.' However, I didn't know they existed until Senator Long named me to the board." The staff writer described Marguerite as being "a prim and sedate little lady who sat demurely on a cushioned sofa, arranging her skirt precisely in the manner of a child caring for her best party frock."[31]

Marguerite received her appointment to the Louisiana Censorship Board in July, and in September of that year Senator Huey P. Long, who was really responsible for the appointment made by Governor Allen, was assassinated at Baton Rouge. Shortly before his tragic death, Senator Long was in New York visiting with Harry and Marguerite. Then,

according to Marguerite, Huey told them that "he didn't want to go back to New Orleans." Ordinarily, he was excited about getting home, but this time he wanted to remain away.

Huey was having dinner with them at the Williams' apartment, and the Louisiana senator sat with his back to a large window. Marguerite recalled that the shade was up and that "he was a perfect target for anybody." Suddenly the lights went on in an apartment across the alleyway, and Marguerite remarked that Huey ought not to expose himself that way.

"He looked at me in a very strange way," Marguerite said, "and then he said to me: 'No, I'm not worried about being shot up here. Nobody up here is going to take a shot at me.' The way he emphasized 'up here' was frightening. Then two weeks later he was killed."[32]

Harry and Marguerite apparently lost active interest in Louisiana politics with the death of Huey Long. In most instances Harry supported him, and Marguerite followed. They had watched the controversial, magnetic Long win the governorship in 1928, then push through the legislature a constitutional amendment to tax the oil interests and then to use the revenue for highways and education. They observed his impeachment by the lower house in 1929 for bribery and misconduct and knew when he rounded up enough state senators (labeled the "Famous 15") to avoid conviction. Still they watched Long climb upward politically as he was elected to the United States Senate in 1930, while still holding tightly on to the governor's office. Then they saw him rule Louisiana from 1930 to 1934 by alliance with the New Orleans Machine as he sponsored a great highway program and the expansion of the Louisiana State University at Baton Rouge. The highways had been in desperate shape; some of the gummiest clay that was ever devoted to thoroughfare existed in Louisiana. The youth of the state benefitted by the expansive program coming to the State University, while not only Louisiana but the whole South profited from Louisiana's new highways built during the darkest months of the Depression. Magnificent bridges with mighty approaches rose to span that impulsive, too independently minded Mississippi River. Even the hyacinthed quagmires of that paradise the Evangeline country yielded to Huey's well built highways and culverts. Then, too, those with long memories in Louisiana or Washington, D.C., can still remember how winningly convincing his speeches could be. So perhaps it was understandable why Harry and Marguerite backed him until the end.

As to the rest of Huey's story, as United States senator, he failed to obtain President Franklin Roosevelt's backing for his social program. Yet unperturbed, Huey organized in early 1934 a Share Our Wealth Society, promising a homestead allowance of $6,000 and a minimum annual income of $2,500 for every American family. The money would be obtained by a capital levy on large fortunes. Back in Louisiana, he reorganized the state government in 1934-1935, and then abolishing the local government, he created a virtual dictatorship. Next he announced his candidacy for the Presidency in March, 1935. Assassination came in September of that year on the steps of the state capitol at Baton Rouge.[33]

Harry's multiple business interests in lumber, in sugar, in oil, and in banking restrained him from concentrating entirely on the Wedell-Williams Air Service Corporation. Yet aircraft built by the company won the first three places in the Bendix trophy race in 1933 and repeated this performance in the two succeeding years. His business interests also occasionally kept him from his wife, but he always had time for Marguerite. Still it was said that near the end of their eighteen years of marriage, she spent more and more of her time in New Orleans without him. Perhaps she had tried to hold him just a little

too closely—for always Marguerite seemed to be so fond of Harry, and Williams was an independently minded person. Yet always they were agreeable, and Marguerite's regard for him and for the Williams family never wavered.[34]

There had been no invasion of tragedy into the life of Marguerite Clark since her childhood days in the 1890s when she had been orphaned by the deaths of her parents, and left in a greatly reduced financial condition. Life had been kind indeed to her—beauty, fame, great wealth, and a happy marriage had all been hers. She had lived the Cinderella story through the years—and then suddenly it was over.

Nineteen thirty-four had not been a happy year for Harry P. Williams. James R. "Jimmy" Wedell, his partner and "the aviation genius in the rough, pilot extraordinary, and daredevil supreme," crashed to his death in Wedell's small "Gypsy Moth" over Patterson. Jimmy, his friend, and president of the Wedell-Williams Air Service Corporation that they had jointly founded, was gone. Harry P. Williams must have felt in the loss that he had parted with his right arm. Scarcely a year later his pilot, Walter Wedell, Jimmy's brother, and an associate too in the Wedell-Williams Company, died in a plane wreck. Again Williams grieved, but still his work went on, and perhaps his greatest reward for achievement came to him during this period of sadness. Williams was greatly honored when a pursuit plane designed by him was selected in nationwide competition by the U.S. Army Air Service.

Then Harry P. Williams followed his friends in death some twelve months after, going as suddenly and valiantly as they, and happiness for Marguerite in Louisiana ended cruelly and abruptly with the sudden death of her husband.[35] Harry P. Williams was killed along with his pilot Johnnie (Red) Worthen when their plane fell near Baton Rouge, Louisiana, on May 19, 1936.[36]

Williams and Worthen had taken off from the airport some six miles east of the city at about 9:40 p.m. Before they gained much altitude, the plane went into a spin and then into a nose dive. It crashed in a swampy area only four miles from the airport. Before striking the ground, the plane cut a path through trees. The plane was demolished, while the great noise of the crash attracted the attention of persons at the airport. Baton Rouge firemen and policemen rushed to the scene.

The manager of the Baton Rouge airport, R. G. Broussard, said that he did not know whether Worthen or Williams was flying the plane at the time of the crash.

"Johnny warmed up the ship, while Mr. Harry came into the airport building to use a telephone," Broussard related. "Johnny was at the controls when I turned on the lights to let them out of the field, but I do not know whether he stayed at the controls after Mr. Harry got into the plane."[37]

It was reported that Harry's last telephone call had been to Marguerite, calling her at their new house in Patterson which Harry had but recently built for her, not to be concerned about his delay, that he would be home shortly. Both of them had been glad to leave the rambling old Williams mansion in Patterson for the spacious and beautiful white house that faced the Wedell-Williams Airport.

Staggered by the tragic news, Marguerite Clark Williams, according to the press, hurried to Baton Rouge and accompanied the body of her Harry to New Orleans where the funeral was held in the great flower-filled living room of the palatial house of Harry's deceased father, Frank B. Williams, and his mother, Elizabeth Seyburn Williams, at 5120 St. Charles Avenue. Thus it was not in a funeral establishment nor in the remoteness of a church auditorium, but at his mother's home that the service was conducted. Traditionally, Southern funerals had been held in the home where the family ties were strongest, and so it was here. Yet the great house was thrown open to all those who loved Harry. The

spacious front rooms were filled with people and with flowers.

Marguerite garbed in black, with a sable veil which covered her lovely features, sat beside her faithful sister Cora, with her close friends too gathered about her. She controlled her agony with a courage of which Harry might have been proud.

The prince of her story was gone. Once in her single days she had told a writer for *Photoplay* that "I have no desire to have my heart broken, so I always take care not to leave it around or lose it." Despite any precautions she may have previously taken, "her heart was broken in the end," so wrote Edward Wagenknecht in *The Movies in the Age of Innocence*, and he continued: "For I have a very pathetic letter, written to a friend after her husband's death. But she was a lady; she did not 'slop over'; she saw the elements of life in a reasonable relationship to each other."[38]

Marguerite Clark maintained a loyalty to her husband, closed the door to her past career as a finished interlude, "and devoted herself to her home and social interests in New Orleans."[39] So different were their backgrounds: he came from a plantation family who long had lived in Louisiana; he was familiar not only with New Orleans, but with the rural South and its small towns. Williams was at home with the fields, the woodlands, and the marshes of southern Louisiana. There he and his people grew sugar-cane, cut timber, and gained from oil. Yet it was flying that evidently meant most to him, and Williams apparently liked the excitement of it, choosing his associates among those who loved the air as much as he.

Marguerite had worked all of her life. Left in poverty as a child, perhaps she never quite escaped from a subconscious fear of it. Before her marriage, she once declared in an interview:

When a man goes broke he can nearly always borrow some money from a friend, or get a small luncheon with a glass of beer for a nickel; but with a girl it is different. No man can realize what a terrible thing it is for a girl to be without any money. She is far more cruelly at the mercy of the world than any man is. I tell you, it is very necessary for a young woman to be practical.[40]

Her older sister, Cora, knew too the dread of poverty and must have realized that in Marguerite lay musical and dramatic talents, which combined with beauty and charm could and would provide security for the two. Years older, she served as Marguerite's manager, coached her in every detail, and with the zeal of the overprotective "stage mother" she guarded her little sister, as only the most conscientious of chaperones might do, until Marguerite married.[41]

So security came to Marguerite, then wealth, for "with seeming effortlessness she rose to lead billing."[42] Yet there were years of mediocre dressing rooms, smoky Pullman cars on passenger trains, grease paint, and work, work, work. Still as young as she was, much of the labor seemed to be really play, for she loved the stage. "I confess that the stage and the lights and the people, and the fine, sonorous phrases written by a master for me to speak fittingly have a fascination that I cannot forget. I will never be able to forget it," Marguerite Clark told an interviewer at one time.

She loved the stage, but it provided its moments of fear, that motion picture acting alleviated for her. "Moving picture work is the best cure for nervousness that I have ever met," she once said and continued: "I used to go through agonies of terror at rehearsals. Even as recently as *Prunella* I was so frightened that I begged Mr. Ames to let me give up the part, and only his insistence and kindly encouragement kept me up to the mark. And this, mind you, years after I ceased to be a novice. Of course the cause of all this was a self-consciousness that was positively morbid. The films have absolutely cured me of that."[43]

Thus, all her years—since she was sixteen to retirement at thirty-eight—had been spent on the professional stage or in films. Marguerite's life had been different indeed from that of Harry P. Williams. The city of New York was for so many years her home, and although some of her later films were made in Hollywood and she had a house in the Beverly Hills area for a time, she held a feeling of regard for the great city and for a long time lived near Central Park. Yet with her marriage, she learned to love Louisiana and with it amiable Patterson and stimulating New Orleans. So the land of azaleas and camelias became the home that, like Harry Williams, completely took her heart.

It seemed to have been a marriage between the bluebird who, according to dramatist Maurice Maeterlinck, escapes from the world to find happiness at home, and the eagle who never tires of soaring towards lands beyond the horizon. Yet Marguerite loved him. With his death, she was desolate. The gentle Prunella had lost her adventurous Pierrot.

Marguerite Clark liked and respected her long-time employer, Adolph Zukor. In 1937 she returned to California for his twenty-fifth wedding anniversary.
(Film Favorites Collection)

Restless and lonely, Marguerite returned to Hollywood in 1937 on her first visit since leaving the screen. The occasion was the twenty-fifth wedding anniversary of her friend Adolph Zukor—long time president of Paramount Pictures and the man whose film company had propelled her into super-star status during those years between mid-1914 and November, 1919. There, too, she was honored at a banquet given by the Academy of Motion Pictures Arts and Sciences. "Motion picture agents at the time," wrote the *Times-Picayune* of New Orleans, "recalled that Mrs. Williams was the only actress who earned more than $1,000,000 a year."[44]

There was a bravery in Marguerite Clark that apparently sustained her always. Certainly it provided the stamina that brought her fame on the New York stage and later carried her to super-stardom in early motion pictures. So she met her grief bravely and accepted, with a sense of responsibility, election to the presidency of the Wedell-Williams Air Service Corporation—a firm Harry P. Williams had founded. She never knew failure herself. There had been poor plays or inferior film stories, or dramatic vehicles that did not appeal at the box office. But she herself had never failed. So she accepted the presidency of his firm which she inherited, and with good judgment, managed it successfully. The company at that time held a mail contract between New Orleans and Houston. Thus Marguerite, in her new position, served as the first woman executive of an air line, and in operating the Wedell-Williams Aviation Company, she was strictly business as she dealt with any associates. Marguerite was a person with common sense, and in her practicality, she apparently possessed a good business head. Certainly her sister Cora had one, and Cora lived for a time with her in New Orleans after Harry P. Williams's death. So Cora, to a limited degree, may have advised her; undoubtedly a lawyer did, and Marguerite signed no contracts or documents without legal aid.

Soon an opportunity came to sell the Wedell-Williams Air Service to the Eastern Air Lines. The favorable offer appealed to Marguerite, as Eastern Air Lines was fast gaining approval among air-minded travellers in the United States. Despite her business abilities, Marguerite lacked self-confidence, and she welcomed the sale, saying: "I could tell pretty soon that I had no mind to run the service. It wasn't in me. So I sold out to Eastern Air Lines. I made them promise they would take over all the pilots, mechanics, and other employees my husband hired, and they kept their promise to the word."[45]

Harry P. Williams left all of his entire estate to her which included the town house in New Orleans on St. Charles Avenue and the plantation in St. Mary's Parish which bordered Patterson. Yet she did not live at either location long and never returned to Patterson as her home. Still at the town, following the sale of the Wedell-Williams Air Service Corporation, she endowed its former airport as the Harry P. Williams Memorial Airport and financially sustained the creation of the Wedell-Williams Memorial Aviation Museum of Louisiana.[46]

Marguerite Clark Williams and Captain Eddie Rickenbacker, of Eastern Airlines, negotiated in New Orleans when she sold the Wendell-Williams Air Service to his company in 1938. (The Historic New Orleans Collection)

Louisiana was empty without her husband. Marguerite sold her palatial home at 5120 St. Charles Avenue, where she had lived following the death of her father-in-law, Frank B. Williams, giving it up to lease a house on Burdette and Freret Streets. Still lonely, she left New Orleans in 1939 for New York where life had once been so kind. There she made her home once more with her sister, Cora.

Marguerite's life in New York was not one of complete solitude, for still lovely—and only very slightly plumpish—she eventually accepted male attention to the extent of being escorted to social affairs. Yet she did not remarry. Perhaps the memory of dashing Harry Williams was too dear for her to care for anyone to take his place.

Death came at fifty-seven, on September 25, 1940, to Marguerite Clark in the late Indian summer of her life. A cerebral hemorrhage struck with cruel finality at a New York restaurant. The hemorrhage had been preceded immediately by a heart attack which had seized her as she was lunching. Quickly pneumonia followed the cerebral attack, and she died five days later at the Le Roy Sanitarium. Cora, with whom Marguerite shared a penthouse at 50 Central Park West, was with her during her final illness. Her nearest survivor was her sister, and there was another relative, a cousin, Hugh R. Wilson, whose career Marguerite had observed with pride.

The funeral service was held in New York at the Frank E. Campbell Funeral Church. There friends and theatrical associates gathered on Saturday morning, September the twenty-seventh. Among the one hundred and fifty persons attending the services were Hugh R. Wilson, former United States Ambassador to Germany; George Jean Nathan, dramatic critic; Lucy Munroe, singer; and Mr. and Mrs. Richard Barthelmess.

Marguerite's personal friend, Reverend Doctor Nathan A. Seagle, rector of St. Stephen's Protestant

Episcopal Church, Broadway and Sixty-ninth Street, conducted the service. During the Bible reading and the eulogy which followed, the dainty figure lay in an open silver-gray casket surrounded by flowers sent by many of her motion-picture and stage associates. She retained her beauty even in death. Two songs were sung—the first, "Lead Kindly Light" by Mary Lane, a former musical comedy star, and "Nearer My God to Thee" at the conclusion of the service, by Lucy Monroe, formally of the Metropolitan Opera.

Floral pieces were banked high along the walls of the chapel as evidences of the love others bore for the tiny, graceful star who, with blossoms in her hair, had danced so attractively on the stage long ago in *Happyland*. Flowers came from Mary Pickford; Mary Boland; Mr. and Mrs. Adolph Zukor; Mel Ott, baseball star; and Captain and Mrs. Eddie Rickenbacker. After the funeral, a short, private service was held at the Ferncliff Crematory at Ardsley, New York. The ashes of Marguerite Clark were sent to New Orleans where they were placed beside those of her husband at Metaire Cemetery in the marble, Egyptian styled tomb of his family. Beauty rested in every line of the structure. Its iron carved doors each carried a sculptured head of an Egyptian ruler, while on each side of these iron portals was a lotus column of gray marble. It was fitting that she who had been so lovely should rest in a place that was beautiful. In death, Marguerite Clark had returned to the two things she valued so greatly: Harry P. Williams and her adopted Louisiana.

To loyal Cora she bequeathed the bulk of her estate, totally valued in New Orleans on February 21, 1941 at $365,436.50. Still Marguerite did not forget others and left forty-one bequests, ranging from $200 to $6,000 each. The generous gift to Cora was the one way Marguerite could partially recompense the sister who had been her life-long champion and Marguerite's mentor of her single years.

From the time the two first left Ohio until Marguerite's marriage in 1918, Cora had fought her sister's battles. She had been a "stage mother" who had zealously protected Marguerite from would-be ardent suitors. An entire generation of daunted youths had retreated in flight before the "Dragon," who had been Marguerite's manager too and had negotiated contracts and other financial arrangements so advantageously that Marguerite entered marriage a wealthy woman in her own right with no need to worry about her sister's financial security.

It was Cora too who had always provided a home for Marguerite, even though, in the early years, it had only been a small apartment, or, when on tour, a hotel room or, perhaps, a parlor car on a train. For over a score of years she was Marguerite's whole family, principal friend and only manager. Cora had planned for her, aspired for her, and paved the road upon which Marguerite advanced to success. At the end Marguerite did not forget her.

Cora continued to live in her apartment on Central Park West until her death in the 1950's.[47]

Marguerite Clark Williams's one-time home at 5120 St. Charles Avenue in New Orleans. The handsome house, once owned by her father-in-law, Frank B. Williams, is now part of the city library system of New Orleans.

Footnotes: Part I

[1]Moses King, *King's Handbook of the United States* (Buffalo: Moses King Corp., Publishers, 1891-92), p. 677; DeWitt Bodeen, *From Hollywood* (New York: A. S. Barnes & Co., 1976; London: Tantivy Press, 1976), p. 33. Guardian Docket 16, p. 498, Court of Common Pleas, Probate Division, Hamilton County, Ohio, Cincinnati, Ohio 45202.

[2]Ibid.

[3]Marguerite Clark, "A Little of My Life," *Motion Picture Magazine* 15 (July, 1918): 60-63; Bodeen, *From Hollywood*, p. 33; Marguerite Clark, "The Story of My Life," *The Chicago Herald*, June 27, 1913; Robinson Locke Collection, vol. 117, Marguerite Clark, vol. 1, p. 6, New York Public Library (microfilm).

[4]Robinson Locke Collection of Dramatic Scrapbooks, vol. 117, series 1, Marguerite Clark, vol. 1, pp. 2-5, New York Public Library.

[5]George Jean Nathan, "George W. Lederer's Reminiscences," *McClures* 52 (May, 1920): 12; Marguerite Clark, "From Comic Opera to Moving Pictures," *The American Magazine* 84 (July, 1917-December, 1917 [December, 1917]: 42; *New York Times*, Sunday, May 4, 1902, sec. 11, pp. 1-2; ibid., Tuesday, May 6, 1903, 9:4-5; Bodeen, *From Hollywood*, p. 33; *Broadway Magazine*, October, 1901; Locke Collection, Marguerite Clark, "The Story of My Life," *Chicago Herald*, June 27. 1913.

[6]*New York Times*, Sunday, May 4, 1902, sec. 11, pp. 1-2; ibid., Tuesday, May 6, 1902, 9:4-5.

[7]"Marguerite Clark Is Ambitious," news clipping dated May 10, 1902, Robinson Locke Collection of Dramatic Scrapbooks, vol. 117-30, series 1, Marguerite Clark, vol. 1, p. 3, New York Public Library.

[8]New York newspaper clipping, August 17, 1902, title of newspaper not given, Robinson Locke Collection of Dramatic Scrapbooks, vol. 117-30, series 1, Marguerite Clark, vol. I, p 3, New York Public Library.

[9]*New York Times*, January 20, 1903, 9:2.

[10]Ibid.

[11]*New York Times*, March 15, 1903, Part 2:26:2.

[12]Robinson Locke Collection of Dramatic Scrapbooks, vol. 117-30, series 1, Marguerite Clark, vol. 1, p. 9, New York Public Library.

[13]Marguerite Clark, "The Story of My Life," *Chicago Herald*, June 27, 1913; Robinson Locke Collection of Dramatic Scrapbooks, vol. 117, series 1, Marguerite Clark, vol. 2, p. 13, New York Public Library.

[14]Robinson Locke Collection of Dramatic Scrapbooks, vol. 117, series 1, Marguerite Clark, 1:29, 22, 80.

[15]*New York Times*, October 3, 1905, 9:3.

[16]Robinson Locke Collection of Dramatic Scrapbooks, vol. 117, Marguerite Clark, vol. 1, pp. 12, 19; *New York Saturday Mail*, December 2, 1905.

[17]*New York Times*, Sunday, March 11, 1906, pt. 4, sec. 5, p. 5; ibid, March 13, 1906, sec. 9, p. 1.

[18]Marguerite Clark, "Truth to the Stagestruck," *Chicago Record*, March 31, 1912; Robinson Locke Collection of Dramatic Scrapbooks, vols. 112-30, series 1, New York Public Library, p. 91.

[19]*Bob Taylor's Magazine*, 3, no. 1 (April, 1906): 11.

[20]Undated clippings, Robinson Locke Collection of Dramatic Scrapbooks, vol. 117, Marguerite Clark, vol. 1, p. 16.

[21]Ibid.

[22]Robinson Locke Collection of Dramatic Scrapbooks, vol. 117, series 1, Marguerite Clark, vol. 1, p. 28, New York Public Library.

[23]Robinson Locke Collection of Dramatic Scrapbooks, vol. 117, series 1, Marguerite Clark, vol. 1, p. 28, New York Public Library.

[24]Ibid., p. 53.

[25]*New York Times*, Sunday, April 1, 1906, pt. 4, 5:1-2.

[26]Ibid., Sunday, May 27, 1906, pt. 4, p. 6:5.

[27]*New York Times*, Sunday, September 1, 1907, pt. 6, 3:2; *New York Telegraph*, May 2, 1907; Robinson Locke Collection, vol. 117, Marguerite Clark, vol. 1.

[28]*Times-Picayune*, Thursday, September 26, 1940, 1:5; 2:3.

[29]Marguerite Clark, "Truth to the Stagestruck," *Chicago Record*, March 31, 1912; Robinson Locke Collection of Dramatic Scrapbooks, vols. 117-30, series 1, p. 91, New York Public Library.

[30]*New York Times*, Sunday, December 6, 1908, pt. 6, 9:1-2; ibid., December 4, 1908, 11:4.

[31]*New York Times*, December 4, 1908, 11:4.

[32]Ibid., Sunday, December 6, 1908, pt. 6, 9:6-7.

[33]*New York Times*, Sunday, April 11, 1909, pt. 6, 2:4.

[34]*St. Louis Star*, July 26, 1909; Robinson Locke Collection of Dramatic Scrapbooks, vol. 117, Marguerite Clark, vol. 1, p. 46. New York *Dramatic News*, August 7, 1909.

[35]Ashton Stevens, "Musical Comedy Never Again! Marguerite Clark Tells Ashton Stevens," *Chicago Examiner*, Sunday, June 12, 1910; Robinson Locke Collection of Dramatic Scrapbooks, vol. 117, series 1, Marguerite Clark, vol. 1, pp.;61-62, New York Public Library.

[36]*New York Morning Telegraph*, August 9, 1909; *Pittsburg Dispatch*, October 19, 1909; Robinson Locke Collection of Dramatic Scrapbooks, vol. 117, series 1, Marguerite Clark, vol. 1, pp. 46-47.

[37]*Chicago Journal*, November 13, 1909; Robinson Locke Collection of Dramatic Scrapbooks, vol. 117, series 1, Marguerite Clark, vol. 1, p. 50, New York Public Library.

[38]Ibid.,

[39]*New York Telegraph*, November 25, 1909; Robinson Locke Collection of Dramatic Scrapbooks, vol. 117, series 1, Marguerite Clark, vol. 1, p. 65.

[40]*The Review* (New York), November 27, 1909; *Chicago Tribune*, June 27, 1910; Robinson Locke Collection, vol. 117, Marguerite Clark, vol. 1, pp. 51, 52.

[41]"Honest, Marguerite Hasn't Married in All Her Lifetime," *Chicago Tribune*, June 26, 1910; Robinson Locke Collection, vol. 117, Marguerite Clark, vol. 1, p. 64.

[42]*The Review* (New York), December 5, 1909; Robinson Locke Collection of Dramatic Scrapbooks, vol. 117, series 1, Marguerite Clark, vol. 1, p. 61, New York Public Library; Ashton Stevens, "Musical Comedy? Never Again" Marguerite Clark tells Ashton Stevens, *Chicago Examiner*, June 12, 1916.

[43]*New York Times*, January 11, 1910, 9:4; "At the Playhouse," *Theatre Magazine*, February 1910, p. 38.

[44]*New York Times*, Sunday, January 16, 1910, pt. 6, 9:2.

[45]Marguerite Clark, "A Little of My Life," *Motion Picture Magazine* 15 (July, 1918): 60-63; *National Cyclopedia of American Biography*, XXX, 328-29.

[46]*New York Times*, May 11, 1910, 9:1

[47]Ibid., Sunday, May 15, 1910, pt. 6, 9:3.

[48]*New York Times*, Sunday, September 11, 1910, pt. 6, 6:4; ibid., Sunday, September 18, 1910, pt. 6, 3:3; *Billboard*, August 20, 1910.

[49]*New York Times*, August 24, 1910, 9:1.

[50]Ibid., Sunday, December 18, 1910, pt. 6, 8:1.

[51]Marguerite Clark, "A Little of My Life," *Motion Picture Magazine* 15 (July, 1918): 60-63.

[52]*New York Times*, May 2, 1911, 11:1.

[53]*The Review* (New York), May 20, 1911; Robinson Locke Collection of Dramatic Scrapbooks, vol. 117, series 1, Marguerite Clark, vol. 1, p. 85, New York Public Library.

[54]Marguerite Clark, "Truth to the Stagestruck," *Chicago Record*, March 31, 1912; Robinson Locke Collection of Dramatic Scrapbooks, vol. 117, series 1, Marguerite Clark, vol. 1, p. 19, New York Public Library.

[55]Robinson Locke Collection of Dramatic Scrapbooks, vol. 117, series 1, Marguerite Clark, vol. 1, New York Public Library; *Toledo Blade*, August 30, 1911.

[56]Marguerite Clark, "A Little of My Life," *Motion Picture Magazine* 15 (July, 1918): 60-63.

[57]*New York Times*, October 15, 1912, 15:1.

[58]"Well, What Might Happen?" *Globe* (New York), December 18, 1912; Robinson Locke Collection, vol. 117, series 1, Marguerite Clark, vol. 1, p. 101.

[59]*New York Times*, November 8, 1912, 13:3.

[60]*New York Times*, May 2, 1913, 11:3.

[61]*New York Telegraph*, May 11, 1913; Robinson Locke Collection, vol. 117, Marguerite Clark, vol. 2, p. 12.

[62]Newspaper clipping, no date; Robinson Locke Collection of Dramatic Scrapbooks, vols. 117-30, series 1, Marguerite Clark, vol. 2, p. 12, New York Public Library.

[63]*New York Times*, October 17, 1913, 11:4.

[64]"Music and Drama. 'Prunella'—A Fantasy of Love in a Dutch Garden," *Current Opinion* 56 (January-June 1914): 24-28.

[65]*New York Times*, October 27, 1913, 9:1.

[66]Marguerite Clark, "A Little of My Life," *Motion Picture Magazine* 15 (July, 1918): 60-63.

Footnotes: Part II

[1]Marguerite Clark, "A Little of My Life," *Motion Picture Magazine* 15 (July 1918): 60-63.

[2]Adolph Zukor, *The Public Is Never Wrong* (New York: G. Putnams' Sons, 1953), p. 113.

[3]Marguerite Clark, "From Comic Opera to Moving Pictures," *American Magazine* 84 (July-December, 1917): 42.

[4]Joe Franklin, *Classics of the Silent Screen* (New York: Bramhall House, 1959), p. 147; Charles Kenmore Ulrich, ed., *Press Book and Advertising Aids, Marguerite Clark in "Wildflower,"* A Paramount Picture, Success Series, Famous Players-Lasky Corporation, Adolph Zukor, President; Jesse L. Lasky, Vice-President; Cecil B. De Mille, Director General, New York, 1919; *The Theatre* 22 (1914): 297.

[5]Adolph Zukor, *The Public Is Never Wrong* (New York: G. P. Putnam's Sons, 1953), p. 127; De Witt Bodeen, "Marguerite Clark," *Films in Review* 15, no. 10 (December 1964): 611; Daniel Blum, *A Pictorial History of the Silent Screen* (New York: Grosset & Dunlap, 1953), p. 53.

[6]Arthur Marx, *The Biography of the Man Behind the Myth, Goldwyn* (New York: W. W. Norton & Co., 1976), p. 63; Carol Easton, *The Search for Sam Goldwyn, a Biography* (New York: William Morrow & Co., 1976), p. 36; Jesse Lasky, *I Blow My Own Horn* (Garden City, N.Y.: Doubleday & Co., 1957), pp. 120-21.

[7]Zukor, *The Public Is Never Wrong*; Bodeen, "Marguerite Clark," p. 622; *The Moving Picture World*, February 6, 1915, p. 808.

[8]*Everybody's Magazine* 33 (July-December, 1915): 48.

[9]Bodeen, "Marguerite Clark," pp. 615, 622-23.

[10]*The Moving Picture World*, June 12, 1915, p. 1787.

[11]*The Moving Picture World*, September 4, 1915.

[12]*New York Times*, November 8, 1915, p. 13, c. 5.

[13]Ibid., November 29, 1915, p. 11, c. 3.

[14]Marguerite Clark, "From Comic Opera to Moving Pictures," *American Magazine* 74 (December, 1917): 42.

[15]*Cosmopolitan* 59, no. 1 (June, 1915): 72.

[16]George Vaux Bacon, "Little Miss Practicality," *Photoplay*, March, 1916, pp. 34-38; Marguerite Clark, "A Little of My Life," *Motion Picture Magazine* 15 (July, 1918): 60-63.

[17]*New York Times*, September 12, 1915, p. 1, col. 4.

[18]Ibid., p. 5, cols. 2, 3.

[19]Adolph Zukor, *The Public Is Never Wrong* (New York: G. P. Putnam's Sons, 1953), p. 140.

[20]*New York Times*, September 14, 1915, p. 11, col. 1.

[21]Vachel Lindsay, *The Art of the Moving Picture* (New York: Macmillan Co., 1916), pp. 28-29.

[22]Bacon, "Little Miss Practicality," p. 40.

[23]George Jean Nathan, *The Entertainment of a Nation* (New York: Alfred A. Knopf, 1942), p. 210.

[24]*Moving Picture World*, January 15, 1916, p. 440; ibid., March 18, 1916, p. 1852; *Motion Picture News*, December 2, 1916.

[25]*New York Times*, April 17, 1916, p. 9, col. 3.

[26]George Blaisdell, "Silks and Satins," *Moving Picture World*, June 24, 1916, p. 2260.

[27]*New York Times*, August 14, 1916, p. 9, col. 5.

[28]Ibid., November 20, 1916, p. 11, col. 1.

[29]*American Magazine*, September, 1916, 82 (New York: Crowell Publishing Co.), p. 33.

[30]*American Magazine* 80, no. 6 (December, 1915): 33.

[31]"The Two Most Popular Women in America," *Everybody's Magazine* 34 (January-June, 1916): 782-84.

[32]Edward Wagenknecht, *The Movies in the Age of Innocence* (Norman: University of Oklahoma Press, 1962), p. 227.

[33]Richard Schickel, *The Disney Version* (New York: Simon & Schuster, 1968), p. 60.

[34]Ibid., p. 231.

[35]George Blaisdell, "Snow White," *The Moving Picture World*, January 6, 1917, p. 97.

[36]Ibid., p. 97; *Motion Picture News*, January 6, 1917, p. 113; *The Moving Picture World*, January 6, 1917, p. 97.

[37]Maude Cheatham, "When Marguerite Says Good-bye!" *Motion Picture Classic* 9 (October, 1919): 18-19.

[38]*The Moving Picture World*, March 3, 1917, pp. 1590-91; *Los Angeles Times*, March 6, 1917, pt. 2.

[39]George Blaisdell, "The Valentine Girl," *The Moving Picture World*, May 5, 1917, p. 808; *The Los Angeles Times*, May 5, 1917, pt. 2, p. 8.

[40]*Los Angeles Times*, August 8, 1917, pt. 2, p. 3.

[41]Louis Reeves Harrison, "Bab's Diary," *The Moving Picture World*, October 27, 1917, p. 520; *Motion Picture News*, October 27, 1917.

[42]*The Moving Picture World*, November 17, 1917, p. 1035; *The Motion Picture News*, November 2, 1917.

[43]De Witt Bodeen, "Marguerite Clark," *Films in Review*, p. 624; *Theatre Magazine* 26, no. 21 (November 1, 1917): 316.

[44]*The Moving Picture World*, January 19, 1918, p. 413.

[45]Barbara Geiman, ed., *Photoplay Treasury* (New York: Crown Publishers, 1972), p. 15.

[46]Lewis Jacobs, *The Rise of the American Film* (New York: Teachers College Press, 1967), p. 255.

[47]*National Cyclopedia of American Biography*, 30:328-29.

[48]*Dramatic Mirror*, November 3, 1917; Marguerite Clark, (1) Portfolio of Clippings and (2) Loose Clippings Ca. 1901-1940, Microfilm, New York Public Library.

[49]*Motion Picture Classic* 5 (October 1917): 45.

[50]Daniel Blum, *A Pictorial History of the Silent Screen* (New York: Grosset & Dunlap, 1953), p. 153.

[51]Ibid.

[52]Jacobs, *The Rise of the American Film*, p. 217.

[53]Wagenknecht, *The Movies in the Age of Innocence*, p. 226.

[54]Ibid.; Lily Jackson, "The Actress and the Aviator," *The Times-Picayune*, October 24, 1976, sec. 4, p. 1; De Witt Bodeen, *From Hollywood* (South Brunswick and New York: A. S. Barnes & Co.; London: Tantivy Press, 1976), p. 31.

[55]Adolph Zukor, *The Public Is Never Wrong* (New York: G. P. Putnam's Sons, 1953), pp. 6-7.

[56]Ibid., pp. 112-14; Lily Jackson, "The Actress and the Aviator," *Times-Picayune*, October 24, 1976, sec. 4, p. 1; interview with General Kemper Williams, July, 1953.

[57]Marguerite Clark, "A Little of My Life," *Motion Picture Magazine* 15 (July, 1918): 60-63; Lily Jackson, "The Actress and the Aviator," October 24, 1976, sec. 4, p. 1.

[58]Jacobs, *The Rise of the American Film*, pp. 217-18.

[59]*The Moving Picture World*, April 20, 1918, p. 437.

[60]*New York Times*, June 3, 1918, p. 9, col. 3.

[61]Jacobs, *The Rise of the American Film*, p. 208.

[62]Wagenknecht, *The Movies in the Age of Innocence*, p. 228.

[63]*New York Times*, June 3, 1918, p. 9, col. 3.

[64]*Everybody's Magazine* 39 (September, 1918) (July-December, 1918), p. 23.

[65]William S. Hart, *My Life East and West* (New York: Blom, 1968), p. 283.

[66]Dorothy Nutting, "With the Newest 'Uncle Tom's Cabin' Company," *Motion Picture Magazine*, September, 1918, pp. 45, 46, 128. In the mid-1930s a clever cartoon comedy *Uncle Tom's Bungalow* was released in which the cowering Uncle Tom told Legree, "You can have my body, but my soul belongs to Warner Brothers."

[67]*Moving Picture World*, September 20, 1918, p. 453.

[68]Zukor, *The Public Is Never Wrong*, p. 112.

[69]*New York Times*, July 26, 1918, p. 11, col. 2

[70]*New York Times*, August 16, 1918, p. 5, col. 2; *National Cyclopedia of American Biography*, 27:61.

[71]*Moving Picture World*, September 28, 1918, p. 1926.

[72]De Witt Bodeen, "Marguerite Clark's Films," *Films in Review* 15 (Dec. 1964): 624.

[73]*Los Angeles Times*, January 28, 1919, pt. 2, p. 3.

[74]Zukor, *The Public Is Never Wrong*, p. 130; De Witt Bodeen, *From Hollywood* (New York: A. S. Barnes, 1976), p. 37.

[75]Herbert Corey, "Money in the Movies," *Everybody's Magazine*, September, 1919 (July-December, 1919), p. 32.

[76]Maude Cheatham, "When Marguerite Says Good-bye," *Motion Picture Classic* 9 (October, 1919): 18-19.

[77]Ibid.

[78]Ibid.

[79]De Witt Bodeen, "Marguerite Clark," *Films in Review* 15, no. 10 (December, 1964): 619; Jesse L. Lasky, *I Blow My Own Horn*, pp. 125-26.

[80]Cheatham, "When Marguerite Says Good-bye," pp. 18-19.

[81]"The Screen," *New York Times*, February 17, 1919, p. 11, cols. 3, 4.

[82]Louis Reeves Harrison, *The Moving Picture World*, March 1, 1919, pp. 1242-43.

[83]"The Screen," *New York Times*, February 18, 1919, p. 11, cols. 3, 4.

[84]"The Screen," *New York Times*, March 31, 1919, p. 11, col. 3; Anthony Anderson, *Los Angeles Times*, April 8, 1919, pt. 3, p. 4; *Moving Picture World*, April 12, 1919, pp. 1242-43.

[85]Bodeen, "Marguerite Clark," p. 625.

[86]"The Screen," May 12, 1919, p. 11, col. 4; *Moving Picture World*, May 24, 1919.

[87]Statement of Mrs. Eleanor Bright Richardson to W. C. Nunn, September 28, 1978.

[88]Bodeen, "Marguerite Clark," p. 625.

[89]"The Screen," *New York Times*, September 22, 1919, p. 8, col. 1.

[90]Jack Mulhall to Wm. Curtis Nunn, June 9, 1978.

[91]*Moving Picture World*, February 14, 1920, pp. 1114-15.

[92]DeWitt Bodeen, "Marguerite Clark's Films," *Films in Review* 15 (1964): 625.

[93]Frederick Lewis Allen, *Only Yesterday, An Informal History of the Nineteen Twenties* (New York: Harper & Brother, Publishers, 1957), p. 13.

Footnotes: Part III

[1]*Times-Picayune*, September 26, 1940, 1:5, 2:3.

[2]Frederick James Smith, "The Lilliput Lady," *Motion Picture Classic* 12 (July, 1921): 44-45.

[3]Ibid.

[4]Lily Jackson, "The Actress and the Aviator," *Times-Picayune*, October 24, 1976, sec. 4, p. 1.

[5]"The Screen," *New York Times*, May 23, 1921, p. 16, col. 3.

[6]Edward Weitzel, review of *Scrambled Wives*, *The Moving Picture World*, May 19, 1921, p. 1502.

[7]*New York Times*, September 26, 1940; Jackson, "The Actress and the Aviator," p. 1.

[8]Marguerite Clark, "The Disadvantages of Being Girlish," *The Theatre*, The Magazine for Playgoers, April, 1914, pp. 188-92.

[9]*Times-Picayune*, September 26, 1940, 1:5, 2:3; New York *Mirror* (Sunday *Mirror* Magazine Section, July 8, 1934).

[10]Interview with Smith Ballew by W. C. Nunn, October 21, 1976.

[11]*Times-Picayune*, September 26, 1940, 1:5, 2:3; Beatrice Washburn, "Marguerite Clark—Today," *Photoplay*, April, 1925, p. 28.

[12]Interview of W. C. Nunn with Mrs. Landry, October 12, 1978; interview of W. C. Nunn with Betty Williams on October 10, 1978.

[13]Arthur Burton La Cour, *New Orleans Masquerade* (New Orleans: Pelican Publishing Co., 1952), p. 187; *Times-Picayune*, September 26, 1940, 1:5, 2:3.

[14]*Times-Picayune*.

[15]La Cour, *New Orleans Masquerade*, p. 187.

[16]Washburn, "Marguerite Clark—Today," pp. 28, 29, 132. Bodeen, *From Hollywood*, pp. 40-41.

[17]Washburn, "Marguerite Clark—Today," pp. 133-34.

[18]Letter of Mrs. Zuma Y. Salaun to W. C. Nunn, October 18, 1978.

[19]*Times-Picayune*, May 20, 1936, p. 1, col. 1; p. 2, col. 3; June 29, 1959, sec. 3, p. 2, cols. 1-3; November 1, 1953, mag. sec., p. 12.

[20]*Times-Picayune*, March 30, 1930, p. 8, col. 6; *National Cyclopedia of American Biography*, vol. 27, p. 61.

[21]*Times-Picayune*, May 27, 1928; June 27, 1928; July 15, 1928; *National Cyclopedia of American Biography*, vol. 27, p. 61.

[22]New Orleans *Sport Times*, October 19, 1931; Peterson Scrapbook, Wedell-Williams Memorial Aviation Museum of Louisiana; *Times-Picayune*, October 19, 1930, October 26, 1931; October 27, 1931.

[23]*National Cyclopedia of American Biography*, vol. 27, p. 61; Jackson, "The Actress and the Aviator," p. 1.

[24]*New Orleans Tribune*, August 10, 1929; Account in Peterson's Scrapbook, Wedell-Williams Memorial Aviation Museum of Louisiana.

[25]Interviews by the author with Betty Williams, October 4, 1978; Anne Cane Brown, Frank B. Williams, Janet W. Yancey, and Eleanor Bright Richardson, September 26, 1978.

[26]*New York World-Telegram*, September 1, 1932, p. 8, cols. 2 and 3.

[27]*New York Telegraph*, October 10, 1933; Loose clippings of Marguerite Clark, ca. 1901-1940, New York Public Library.

[28]*New York Times*, July 16, 1935, 22:4.

[29]*Times-Picayune*, September 26, 1940, 1:5; 2:3.

[30]*New York World-Telegram*, August 21, 1935, p. 16, cols. 1, 3, 4; Bodeen, *From Hollywood*, pp. 41-42.

[31]*New York World-Telegram*, August 21, 1935, p. 16, cols. 1, 2, 3, 4.

[32]Elliott Arnold, "Marguerite Clark, an Old Friend of Huey Long, Hears His Horse-Laugh at His Brother's Downfall," *New York World-Telegram*, March 2, 1940; Loose Clippings of Marguerite Clark, ca. 1901-1940 (microfilm), New York Public Library.

[33]Richard B. Morris, *Encyclopedia of American History* (New York: Harper & Row Publishers, 1965), p. 745.

[34]Interview by the author with Eleanor Bright Richardson, September 26, 1978.

[35]*New York Times*, May 21, 1936, p. 5, col. 1; New Orleans *Times-Picayune*, May 20, 1936, p. 1, col. 1; p. 2, col. 3; *National Cyclopedia of American Biography*, vol. 27, p. 61.

[36]*Times-Picayune*, May 20, 1936, p. 1, col. 1; p. 2, col. 1; *New York Times*, September 26, 1940.

[37]*Times-Picayune*, May 20, 1936, p. 1.

[38]*Photoplay*, March, 1916, p. 35; Edward Wagenknecht, *The Movies in the Age of Innocence*, p. 228.

[39]*New York Times*, May 21, 1936, p. 5, col. 1.

[40]*Photoplay*, March, 1916, p. 38.

[41]Zukor, *The Public Is Never Wrong*, p. 112.

[42]Ibid.

[43]Marguerite Clark, "From Comic Opera to Moving Pictures," *The American Magazine* 84 (July, 1917-December, 1917): 42.

[44]*Times-Picayune*, September 26, 1940, p. 1, col. 5; p. 2, col. 3.

[45]Arnold, "Marguerite Clark, an Old Friend of Huey Long Hears His Horse-Laugh at His Brother's Downfall"; Statement of Anne Cane Brown to W. C. Nunn, September 26, 1978; *New York Times*, September 26, 1940, Obituaries, L. 23.

[46]*New York Times*, September 26, 1940, Obituaries, L. 23; Lily Jackson, "The Actress and the Aviator," p. 2; *New York Herald Tribune*, September 26, 1940, p. 18, cols. 2-3.

[47]*New York Times*, September 29, 1940, p. 43, col. 2; *New York Herald Tribune*, September 29, 1940, p. 36, col. 7; *New York Times*, February 22, 1941; *Portfolio of Clippings and Loose Clippings of Marguerite Clark*, ca. 1901-1940 (microfilm), New York Public Library.

Bibliography: Primary Sources

AUTOBIOGRAPHICAL MATERIALS

Clark, Marguerite. "The Disadvantages of Being Girlish." *The Theatre*, April, 1914, pp. 188-92.

_____. "From Comic Opera to Moving Pictures." *The American Magazine* 84 (July, 1917-December, 1917): 42.

_____. "A Little of My Life." *Motion Picture Magazine* 15 (July, 1918): 60-63.

_____. "The Story of My Life." *The Chicago Herald*, June 27, 1913.

_____. "Truth to the Stagestruck." *Chicago Record*, March 31, 1912.

COLLECTIONS

Clark, Marguerite. (1) Portfolio of clippings, and (2) loose clippings, ca. 1901-1940. Microfilm, New York Public Library.

Robinson Locke Collection of Dramatic Scrapbooks, vol. 117, series 1, Marguerite Clark, vol. 1. Microfilm, New York Public Library.

DOCUMENTS

Catalogue of Copyright Entries, Motion Pictures 1912-1939. Copyright Office, Library of Congress, Washington, D.C., 1951.

Guardian Docket 16, p. 498, Court of Common Pleas, Probate Division, Hamilton County Ohio, Cincinnati, Ohio.

INTERVIEWS AND LETTERS

Ballew, Smith. Interviews, October 21, 1976, and September 21, 1978.

Brown, Anne Cane. Statement, September 26, 1978.

Landry, Helen B. Patterson, Louisiana. Statement, October 12, 1978.

Muhall, Jack. Note, October 18, 1978.

Richardson, Eleanor Bright. Statements, September 26, 1978, and September 28, 1978.

Salaun, Zuma Y. Letter, October 18, 1978.

Williams, Betty. Statements, October 4, 1978, and October 10, 1978.

Williams, Frank B. Statement, September 26, 1978.

Williams, General L. Kemper. Williams, Inc., 1323 Whitney Building, New Orleans, Louisiana. Interview, July 21, 1953.

Yancey, Janet W. Statement, September 26, 1978.

ARTICLES

Arnold, Elliott. "Marguerite Clark, an Old Friend of Huey Long, Hears His Horse-Laugh at His Brother's Downfall." *New York World-Telegram*, March 12, 1940.

"At the Playhouse." *Theatre*, February, 1910, p. 38.

Bacon, George Vaux. "Little Miss Practicality." *Photoplay*, March, 1916, pp. 34-38.

Bob Taylor's Magazine 3, no. 1 (April, 1906): 11.

Cheatham, Maude. "When Marguerite Says Good-Bye." *Motion Picture Classic* 9 (October, 1919): 18-19.

Corey, Herbert. "Money in the Movies." *Everybody's Magazine*, September, 1919 (July-December, 1919), p. 32.

Dale, Alan. "Only Play Acting." *Cosmopolitan* 59, no. 1 (June, 1915): 72.

"Movie Actors Make More Money Than the President of the United States." *The American Magazine* 82 (September 1916): 33.

"Music and Drama. 'Prunella'—A Fantasy of Love in a Dutch Garden." *Current Opinion* 56 (January-June, 1914): 24-28.

Nathan, George Jean. "George W. Lederer's Reminiscences." *McClure's* May, 1920, p. 52.

"Salaries of the Stars." *Everybody's Magazine* 39 (July-December 1918): 23.

Smith, Frederick James. "The Lilliput Lady." *Motion Picture Classic* 12 (July, 1921): 44-45.

"Stage Actors and Actresses Turn to the Movies." *The American Magazine* 80 (December, 1915): 33.

Stevens, Ashton. "Musical Comedy Never Again! Marguerite Clark Tells Ashton Stevens." *Chicago Examiner*, June 12, 1910.

"The Two Most Popular Women in America." *Everybody's Magazine* 34 (January-June, 1916): 782-84.

Washburn, Beatrice. "Marguerite Clark—Today." *Photoplay*, April, 1925, p. 28.

MAGAZINES

American Magazine 80 (December, 1915): 33; 82 (September, 1916) 33; 84 (July-December, 1917), 42.

Bob Taylor's Magazine 3, no. 1 (April, 1906): 11.

Cosmopolitan 59, no. 1 (June, 1915): 72.

Current Opinion 56 (January-June, 1914): 24-28.

Everybody's Magazine 33 (July-December, 1915): 48; 34 (January-June, 1916): 782-784; 39 (July-December, 1918): 23; 41 (July-December, 1919): 32.

McClure's, (May, 1920): 52.

Motion Picture Classic 5 (October, 1917): 45; 9 (October, 1919): 18-19; 12 (July, 1921): 44-45.

Motion Picture Magazine, July, 1918: pp. 60-63; September, 1918, pp. 45, 46, 128.

Motion Picture News, December 2, 1916, p. 110; January 6, 1917, p. 113.

The Moving Picture World, February 6, 1915, p. 808; June 12, 1915, p. 1787; September 4, 1915, p. 409; January 15, 1916, p. 440; March 18, 1916, p. 1852; June 24, 1916, p. 2260; January 6, 1917, p. 97; March 3, 1917, pp. 1590-91; May 5, 1917, p. 808; January 19, 1918, p. 413; April 20, 1918, p. 453; September 23, 1918, p. 1926; March 1, 1919, pp. 1242-43; May 24, 1919, p. 1225; February 14, 1920, pp. 1114-15; May 18, 1921, p. 1502.

Photoplay, March, 1916, pp. 34-38; April, 1925, p. 28.

Theatre, February, 1910, p. 38; April, 1914, pp. 188-192; November 1, 1917, p. 316.

NEWSPAPERS

Chicago Journal, November 13, 1909.

Chicago Record, March 31, 1912.

Chicago Tribune, June 26, 1910; June 27, 1910.

Dramatic News (New York), August 7, 1909.

The Globe (New York), December 18, 1912.

The Los Angeles Times, August 1, 1915, part 3:3, August 22, 1915, part 3:3; November 7, 1915, part 3:3; January 27, part 2:6; January 5, 1916, part 2:6; January 16, 1916, part 3:3; April 9, 1916, part 3A:21; April 16, 1916, part 3A:21; April 23, 1916, part 3A:18; May 1, 1916, part 2:8; June 18, 1916, part 3A:18; August 3, 1916, part 3:19; March 6, 1917, part 2:16; May 5, 1917, part 2:8; August 8, 1917, part 2:3.

New Orleans Sport Times, October 19, 1931.

Times-Picayune (New Orleans), May 27, 1928; June 27, 1928; July 15, 1928; March 30, 1930, 8, col. 6; October 26, 1931; October 27, 1931; May 20, 1936, 1, col. 1; 2, col. 3; September 26, 1940, 1:5, 2:3; November 1, 1953, mag. sec. 12; June 29, 1959, sec. 3, part 3:2, cols. 1-3; October 24, 1976, sec. 4, p. 1.

The New Orleans Tribune, August 10, 1929.

New York Herald Tribune, September 26, 1940; 18, cols. 2-3; September 29, 1940, 36, col. 7.

New York Mirror, Sunday Mirror magazine section, July 8, 1934.

The New York Telegraph, May 2, 1907; August 9, 1909; November 25, 1909; May 11, 1913.

The New York Times, May 4, 1902, 11:1-2; May 6, 1902, 9:4-5; January 20, 1903, 9:2; March 15, 1903, part 2:26:2; October 23, 1905, 9:3; March 11, 1906, part 4:5:5; March 13, 1906, 9:1; April 1, 1906, part 4:5:1-2; May 27, 1906, part 4:6:5; December 6, 1908, part 6:9:1-2; December 4, 1908, 11:4; September 1, 1907, part 6:3:2; December 6, 1908, part 6:9:6-7; April 11, 1909, part 6:2:4; January 11, 1910, 9:4; January 16, 1910, part 6, 9:2; May 11, 1910, 9:1; May 15, 1910, part 6, 9:3; September 11, 1910, part 6:6:4; September 18, 1910, part 6:3:3; August 24, 1910, 9:1; December 18, 1910, part 6:8:1; May 2, 1911, 11:1; October 15, 1912, 15:1; November 8, 1912, 13:3; May 2, 1913, 11:3; October 17, 1913, 11:4; October 27, 1913, 9:1; September 14, 1915, 11:1; November 8, 1915, 13:5; November 29, 1915, 11:3; September 12, 1915, 1:4; 5:2, 3; April 17, 1916, 9:3; August 14, 1916, 9:5; November 20, 1916, 11:1; December 25, 1916, 7:1; June 3, 1918, 9:3; July 26, 1918, 11:2; August 16, 1918, 5:2; February 18, 1919, 11:3, 4; March 31, 1919, 11:3; May 12, 1919, 11:4; September 22, 1919, 3:1; May 23, 1921, 16:3; December 4, 1918, 11:4; July 16, 1935, 22:4; May 20, 1936, 31:4; May 21, 1936, 5:1; September 26, 1940, (Obituaries), L 23; September 29, 1940, 43:2.

Pittsburg Dispatch, October 19, 1909.

The Review (New York), November 27, 1909; December 5, 1909.

St. Louis Star, July 26, 1909.

Toledo Blade, August 30, 1911.

Bibliography: Secondary Sources

BOOKS

Allen, Frederick Lewis. *Only Yesterday, An Informal History of the Nineteen Twenties.* New York: Harper & Brother, Publishers, 1957.

Blum, Daniel. *A Pictorial History of the Silent Screen.* New York: Grosset & Dunlap, 1953.

Bodeen, DeWitt. *From Hollywood.* New York: A. S. Barnes & Co.; London: Tantivy Press, 1976.

Easton, Carol. *The Search for Sam Goldwyn, a Biography.* New York: William Morrow & Co., 1976.

Franklin, Joe. *Classics of the Silent Screen.* New York: Bramhall House, 1959.

Geiman, Barbara, ed. *Photoplay Treasury.* New York: Crown Publishers, 1972.

Hart, William S. *My Life East and West.* New York: B. Blom, 1968.

Jacobs, Lewis. *The Rise of the American Film.* New York: Teachers College Press, 1967.

King, Moses. *King's Handbook of the United States.* Buffalo: Moses King Corporation, Publishers, 1891-92.

La Cour, Arthur Burton. *New Orleans Masquerade.* New Orleans: Pelican Publishing Co., 1952.

Lasky, Jesse. *I Blow My Own Horn.* Garden City, New York: Doubleday & Co., 1957.

Lindsay, Vachel. *The Art of the Moving Picture.* New York: Macmillan, 1916.

Marx, Arthur. *The Biography of the Man Behind the Myth, Goldwyn.* New York: W. W. Norton & Co., 1976.

Morris, Richard B. *Encyclopedia of American History.* New York: Harper & Row, 1965.

Nathan, George Jean. *The Entertainment of a Nation.* New York: Alfred A. Knopf. 1942.

Schickel, Richard. *The Disney Version.* New York: Simon & Schuster, 1968.

Ulrich, Charles Kenmore, ed. *Press Book and Advertising Aids, Marguerite Clark in "Wildflower."* New York: Famous Players-Lasky Corporation, n.d.

Wagenknecht, Edward. *The Movies in the Age of Innocence.* Norman: University of Oklahoma Press, 1962.

Weaver, John T. *Twenty Years of Silents.* Metuchen, New Jersey: The Scarecrow Press, Inc.. 1971.

Zukor, Adolph. *The Public Is Never Wrong.* New York: G. P. Putnam's Sons, 1953.

ARTICLES

Bodeen, De Witt. "Marguerite Clark." *Films in Review* 15, no. 10 (December, 1964): 611-25.

Jackson, Lily. "The Actress and the Aviator." *Times-Picayune* (New Orleans), October 24, 1976, sec. 4, pt. 1.

The Films of Marguerite Clark

FILM	DIRECTOR*	LEADING MAN*	SUPPORTING PLAYERS
1. **WILDFLOWER** (1914) (4 reels) From a story by Mary Germaine *Famous Players (Paramount)*	Allen Dwan	Harold Lockwood	Jack Pickford James Cooley E. L. Davenport
2. **THE CRUCIBLE** (1914) (5 reels) From a story by Mark Lee Luther *Famous Players (Paramount)*	Edwin S. Porter	Harold Lockwood	Justine Johnstone Helen Hall Lucy Parker Barbara Winthrop Clifford Grey Blanche Fisher
3. **THE GOOSE GIRL** (1915) (5 reels) Scenario by Wm. C. de Mille from a novel by Harold McGrath *Jesse L. Lasky Feature Play Co.* *(Paramount)*	Fred Thompson	Monroe Salisbury	Larry Payton S. N. Dunbar Sidney Deane James Neill Page Peters Horace B. Carpenter Ernest Joy Jane Darwell
4. **GRETNA GREEN** (1915) (4 reels) From a comedy by Grace Livingstone Furniss *Famous Players (Paramount)*	Thomas N. Heffron	Wilmuth Merkyl	Arthur Hoops Helen Lutrell
5. **THE PRETTY SISTER OF JOSE** (1915) (5 reels) Based on a story and play by Frances Hodgson Burnett *Famous Players*	Allan Dwan	Rupert Julian	Jack Pickford Teddy Sampson Gertrude Norman Dick Rosson William Lloyd Edythe Chapman

The Films of Marguerite Clark

FILM	DIRECTOR*	LEADING MAN*	SUPPORTING PLAYERS
6. **THE SEVEN SISTERS** (1915) (5 reels) Edith Ella Furness's version of an Hungarian comedy *Famous Players (Paramount)*	Sidney Olcott	Conway Tearle	Lola Barclay Madge Evans Jean Stewart Edwin Mordant George Renevant
7. **HELENE OF THE NORTH** (1915) (5 reels) Scenario by J. Searle Dawley *Famous Players (Paramount)*	J. Searle Dawley	Conway Tearle	Elliot Dexter Frank Losee Brigham Royce Kathryn Adams Ida Darling Theodore Guise
8. **STILL WATERS** (1915) (5 reels) From a story by Edith Bernard Delano *Famous Players (Paramount)*	J. Searle Dawley	Robert Broderick	Robert Vaughn Arthur Evers Robert Conville Ottola Nesmith Phillip Tonge
9. **THE PRINCE AND THE PAUPER** (1915) (5 reels) Scenario by Hugh Ford from the novel by Mark Twain *Famous Players (Paramount)*	Edwin S. Porter Hugh Ford	William Sorelle	William Barrows Robert Broderick William Frederick
10. **MICE AND MEN** (1916) (5 reels) Scenario by Hugh Ford from the play by Madeline Lucette Ryley *Famous Players (Paramount)*	J. Searle Dawley	Marshall Neilan	Charles Waldron Clarence Handysides Maggie Halloway Fisher Robert Conville Helen Dahl

The Films of Marguerite Clark

FILM	DIRECTOR*	LEADING MAN*	SUPPORTING PLAYERS
11. **OUT OF THE DRIFTS** (1916) (5 reels) Scenario by William Clifford *Famous Players (Paramount)*	J. Searle Dawley	William Courtleigh, Jr.	J. W. Johnston Albert Gran Kitty Brown Robert Conville Ivan Simpson
12. **MOLLY MAKE-BELIEVE** (1916) (5 reels) Scenario by Hugh Ford *Famous Players (Paramount)*	J. Searle Dawley	Mahlon Hamilton	Dick Gray Helen Dahl Gertrude Norman Kate Lester J. W. Johnston Edwin Mordant
13. **SILKS AND SATINS** (1916) (5 reels) Scenario by Hugh Ford *Famous Players (Paramount)*	J. Searle Dawley	Vernon Steele	Clarence Handysides W. A. Williams Thomas Holding
14. **LITTLE LADY EILEEN** (1916) (5 reels) Scenario by Hugh Ford *Famous Players (Paramount)*	J. Searle Dawley	Vernon Steele	John L. Shine J. K. Murray Harry Lee Maggie Halloway Fisher Russell Bassett
15. **MISS GEORGE WASHINGTON** (1916) (5 reels) Scenario by Lew Allen *Famous Players (Paramount)*	J. Searle Dawley	Niles Welch	Frank Losee Herbert Prior Florence Martin Joseph Gleason Maude Turner Gordon "Billy" Watson

The Films of Marguerite Clark

FILM	DIRECTOR*	LEADING MAN*	SUPPORTING PLAYERS
16. **SNOW WHITE** (1916) (6 reels) Scenario by Winthrop Ames from his own play (1912) based on the Grimm Brothers tale *Famous Players (Paramount)*	J. Searle Dawley	Creighton Hale	Dorothy Cumming Lionel Braham Alice Washburn
17. **THE FORTUNES OF FIFI** (1917) (5 reels) Scenario by Eve Unsell from the novel by Molly Elliott Sewell *Famous Players (Paramount)*	Robert G. Vignola	William Sorelle	John Sainpolis Kate Lester Yvonne Chevalier Jean Gautier J. K. Murray
18. **THE VALENTINE GIRL** (1917) (5 reels) Scenario by J. Searle Dawley from a story by Laura Sawyer *Famous Players (Paramount)*	J. Searle Dawley	Richard Barthelmess	Frank Losee Kathryn Adams Maggie Halloway Fisher Adolphe Menjou Edith Campbell Walker
19. **THE AMAZONS** (1917) (5 reels) Scenario by Frances Marion from Sir Arthur Wing Pinero's play *Famous Players (Paramount)*	Joseph Kaufman	Jack Standing	Elsie Lawson Helene Greene Adolphe Menjou Edgar Norton William Hinckley Andre Bellon
20. **BAB'S DIARY** (1917) (5 reels) Scenario by Margaret Turnbull from the "Bab" stories by Mary Roberts Rinehart *Famous Players (Paramount)*	J. Searle Dawley	Richard Barthelmess	Nigel Barrie Frank Losee Guy Coombs Helene Greene Isabel O'Madigan Jack O'Brian

The Films of Marguerite Clark

FILM	DIRECTOR*	LEADING MAN*	SUPPORTING PLAYERS
21. **BAB'S BURGLAR** (1917) (5 reels) Scenario by Margaret Turnbull from the "Bab" stories by Mary Roberts Rinehart *Famous Players (Paramount)*	J. Searle Dawley	Richard Barthelmess	Frank Losee Leone Morgan Helene Greene Isabel O'Madigan William Hinckley Guy Coombs
22. **BAB'S MATINEE IDOL** (1917) (5 reels) Scenario by Margaret Turnbull from the "Bab" stories by Mary Roberts Rinehart *Famous Players (Paramount)*	J. Searle Dawley	Nigel Barrie	William Hinckley Frank Losee Helene Greene Leone Morgan
23. **THE SEVEN SWANS** (1917) (5 reels) Scenario by J. Searle Dawley from a fairy tale by Hans Christian Andersen *Famous Players (Paramount)*	J. Searle Dawley	Richard Barthelmess	William Danforth August Anderson Edwin Dennison Jules Raucourt Daisy Belmore
24. **RICH MAN, POOR MAN** (1918) (5 reels) Scenario by J. Searle Dawley from Maximillian Foster's novel and the subsequent theatrical dramatization by George Broadhurts *Famous Players (Paramount)*	J. Searle Dawley	Richard Barthelmess	Frederick Warde George Backus J. W. Herbert Ottola Nesmith Augusta Anderson

The Films of Marguerite Clark

FILM	DIRECTOR*	LEADING MAN*	SUPPORTING PLAYERS
25. **PRUNELLA** (1918) (5 reels) Scenario by Charles Maigne from the play by Granville Barker and Laurence Houseman *Famous Players-Lasky (Paramount)*	Maurice Tourneur	Jules Racourt	Harry Leone Isabel Berwin Marcia Harris Nora Cecil
26. **UNCLE TOM'S CABIN** (1918) (5 reels) Scenario by J. Searle Dawley from the novel by Harriet Beecher Stowe *Famous Players-Lasky (Paramount)*	J. Searle Dawley	Frank Losee	J. W. Johnston Florence Carpenter Walter Lewis August Anderson Ruby Hoffman Henry Stafford Mrs. Priestly Morrison
27. **OUT OF A CLEAR SKY** (1918) (5 reels) Scenario by Marshall Neilan from a novel by Maria Thompson Davies *Famous Players-Lasky (Paramount)*	Marshall Neilan	Thomas Meighan	Bobby Connelly E. J. Radcliffe Raymond Bloomer Robert Dudley W. P. Lewis Maggie Halloway Fisher
28. **LITTLE MISS HOOVER** (1918) (5 reels) Scenario by Adrian Gilspear from the play by Maria Thompson Davies *Famous Players-Lasky (Paramount)*	John S. Robertson	Eugene O'Brien	Alfred Hickman Forrest Baldwin Hal Reid Frances Haye

The Films of Marguerite Clark

FILM	DIRECTOR*	LEADING MAN*	SUPPORTING PLAYERS
29. **MRS. WIGGS OF THE CABBAGE PATCH** (1919) (5 reels) Scenario by Eve Unsell from a play by Alice Hegan Rice and Anne Crawford Flexner *Famous Players-Lasky (Paramount)*	Hugh Ford	Gareth Hughes	Mary Carr Vivia Ogden May McAvoy Gladys Valerie Jack McLean Lawrence Johnson
30. **THREE MEN AND A GIRL** (1919) (5 reels) Scenario by Eve Unsell from the stage comedy by Edward Childs Carpenter *Famous Players-Lasky (Paramount)*	Marshall Neilan	Richard Barthelmess	Percy Marmont Jerome Patrick Ida Darling Charles Craig
31. **LET'S ELOPE** (1919) (5 reels) Scenario by Katherine Reed from Fred Jackson's comedy *The Naughty Wife* *Famous Players-Lasky (Paramount)*	John S. Robertson	Frank Mills	Gaston Glass Helene Greene Blanche Standing George Stevens
32. **COME OUT OF THE KITCHEN** (1919) (5 reels) Scenario by Clara Beranger from A. E. Thomas' dramatization of Alice Duer Miller's story *Famous Players-Lasky (Paramount)*	John S. Robertson	Eugene O'Brien	Frances Kaye Bradley Barker Albert M. Hackett May Kitson George Stevens Frederick Esmelton Crawford Kent Augusta Anderson Rita Spear Frances Grant

The Films of Marguerite Clark

FILM	DIRECTOR*	LEADING MAN*	SUPPORTING PLAYERS
33. **GIRLS** (1919) Scenario by Walter Edwards based on Clyde Fitch's stage comedy *Famous Players-Lasky (Paramount)*	Walter Edwards	Harrison Ford	Helene Chadwick Mary Warren Lee Hill Clarissa Selwyn Arthur Edmund Carew
34. **WIDOW BY PROXY** (1919) (5 reels) Scenario by Julie Crawford Ivors from the play by Catherine Chisholm Cushing *Famous Players-Lasky (Paramount)*	Walter Edwards	Nigel Barrie	Jack Gilbert Brownie Vernon Gertrude Norman Gertrude Claire
35. **LUCK IN PAWN** (1919) (5 reels) Scenario by Alice Eyton from the play by Marvin Taylor *Famous Players-Lasky (Paramount)*	Walter Edwards	Charles Meredith	Leota Lorraine
36. **A GIRL NAMED MARY** (1919) (5 reels) Scenario by Alice Eyton from a story by Juliet Wilbur Tompkins *Famous Players-Lasky (Paramount)*	Walter Edwards	Wallace MacDonald	Kathlyn Williams Aggie Herring Charles Clary Lillian Leighton Pauline Pulliam

The Films of Marguerite Clark

FILM	DIRECTOR*	LEADING MAN*	SUPPORTING PLAYERS
37. **ALL-OF-A-SUDDEN PEGGY** (1919) (5 reels) Scenario by Edith Kennedy from a story by Ernest Denny *Famous Players-Lasky (Paramount)*	Walter Edwards	Jack Mulhall	Oral Humphrey Lillian Leighton Maggie Halloway Fisher Sylvia Jocelyn
38. **EASY TO GET** (1920) (5 reels) Scenario by Julie Crawford Ivers from a story by Mann Page *Famous Players-Lasky (Paramount)*	Walter Edwards	Harrison Ford	Rod La Rocque Helene Greene
39. **SCRAMBLED WIVES** (1921) (6 reels) Scenario by Gardner Hunting from the play by Adelaide Matthews and Martha M. Stanley *Adolph Klauber for Marguerite Clark Productions, Inc. Released by First National*	Edward H. Griffith	Leon P. Gendron	Ralph Bunke Florence Martin Virginia Lee Alice Mann Frank Badgley

The Films of Marguerite Clark

*The directors and leading men for each film deserve brief biographical attention.

1. **WILDFLOWER.** *Director* Allan Dwan was born at Toronto, Canada in 1885 and was believed to be the most prolific director in motion pictures with 1,500 films to his credit. He began with the American Film Co. in 1911, went to Universal in 1918, and on to Famous Players in 1914 where he remained about two years. He next went to Triangle where he directed some of Douglas Fairbank's early films. Dwan's proficiency kept him in constant demand. He directed other Douglas Fairbank's pictures and also some of Gloria Swanson's. Dwan adapted well to sound pictures. His last two films appeared in 1956.

The *leading man,* Harold Lockwood, (1887-1918), was a handsome stock and vaudeville actor who entered the Rex Film Company in 1911 and was never again without a film engagement. He moved on from Rex to Nestor Films and then to Selig. By 1914, he was leading man for Mary Pickford and Marguerite Clark at Famous Players. He gained wide attention as a romantic lead opposite May Allison in *David Harum.* He left Famous Players to team with May Allison in 14 co-starring pictures at the American Film Company. At Metro, they continued to co-star until 1917. He was starring alone when he died in 1918 during the flu epidemic.

2. **THE CRUCIBLE.** Edwin S. Porter, (1869-1941), was born in Souzia, Italy and came to the United States in childhood. He was the first American director of importance, directing *The Great Train Robbery* (Edison, 1903). In the picture, he made the first effective use of the film narrative. He also gave D. W. Griffith his first film acting experience in 1907. Porter founded the Rex Film Company in 1909 and made a number of films there. He joined Famous Players in 1912 and directed Mary Pickford in her well known *Tess of the Storm Country* in 1914. Porter retired from film making in 1915 after directing *The Eternal City* (Famous Players) starring Pauline Frederick at Rome. The *leading man* in *The Crucible* was Harold Lockwood.

3. **THE GOOSE GIRL.** Fred Thompson, *director,* came to Jesse L. Lasky Feature Play Co. in 1913. He was a popular and efficient director whose artistic sense made *The Goose Girl* pictorially beautiful. *Leading man.* Monroe Salisbury was a leading man for the Jesse L. Lasky Feature Play Co. who supported Bessie Barriscale in *The Rose of the Rancho* (1914). Salisbury had earlier gained the attention of the producer Jesse L. Lasky as a featured actor in *The Squaw Man.* He was starring for Universal by 1918.

4. **GRETNA GREEN.** *Director.* Thomas N. Heffron was one of the able, early directors for Famous Players and directed John Barrymore in *The Man from Mexico* (1914) and *Are You a Mason?* (1915). Harold Lockwood received Heffron's direction at Famous Players in *The Scales of Justice* (1914). After *Gretna Green,* one of his better pictures was *The Prodigal Liar* (Robertson-Cole, 1919) with Betty Compson and William Desmond. *Leading Man.* Wilmuth Merkyl was employed for a brief time to play supporting roles at Famous Players in New York. That same year (1915) he went to Kalem film company, but the organization soon ceased to exist as it resisted moving from two reel picture making to producing films of five or more reels in length.

5. **THE PRETTY SISTER OF JOSE.** Allan Dwan, *director.* Rupert Julian, *leading man,* although capable as a lead, gave up acting for directing. He directed many features for Universal and gained fame for completing *The Merry-go-Round* in 1923. He is well remembered for his direction of Lon Chaney in *The Phantom of the Opera* (1925).

6. **THE SEVEN SISTERS.** Director Sidney Olcott went to work for Biograph in 1904 but moved to Kalem to direct in 1906. The next year he made a one reel *Ben Hur* which was an innovation in the American cinema. Among his best films were *Monsieur Beaucaire* (Paramount, 1924) starring Rudolph Valentino, *The Charmer* (Paramount, 1925) with Pola Negri as star, and *Ransom's Folly* (First National, 1926) with Richard Barthelmess in the starring role. *Leading man* Conway Tearle had played leads on the New York stage with Grace George in *The Truth* (1914) and Ethel Barrymore in *The Nightingale* (1914) and in Alco Films before playing opposite Marguerite Clark in *The Seven Sisters.* He moved easily back and forth between stage and screen and again was leading man for Ethel Barrymore on Broadway in 1917. On the screen he played leads with Mary Pickford, Norma Talmadge, Constance Talmadge, Pola Negri, Barbara La Marr and many others. Later on the New York stage, he was leading man to Tallulah Bankhead in *Antony and Cleopatra.*

7. **HELENE OF THE NORTH.** J. Searle Dawley, *director,* was one of Famous Players' most proficient directors, establishing himself in 1913 as co-director with Edwin S. Porter of *In the Bishop's Carriage,* starring Mary Pickford. He then directed another Mary Pickford picture, *Caprice* (1913) and *An American Citizen* (1914) with John Barrymore as star. J. Searle Dawley directed Marguerite Clark in sixteen motion pictures. His knowledge of dramatic values, his imagery, and his artistry as evidenced in *Snow White* (1916), starring Marguerite Clark, were praised by the

Motion Picture World in January, 1917. Many of Dawley's earlier films were directed at New York City in the Famous Players studio on 26th street. *Leading Man,* Conway Tearle.

8. **STILL WATERS.** Director, J. Searle Dawley. *Leading man* Robert Broderick was an actor who played character roles or leads with equal versatility. He was the good looking doctor of *Still Waters* and, shortly after, the burly Henry VIII of *Prince and the Pauper.*

9. **THE PRINCE AND THE PAUPER.** *Directors,* Edwin S. Porter and Hugh Ford. Edwin S. Porter left for Italy to direct *The Eternal City* (1915), and Hugh Ford did much of the directing of this picture. Hugh Ford was considered to be a principal director of the Famous Players, New York studio. He participated with Edwin S. Porter in directing *The Crucible* with Marguerite Clark in 1914, and he directed Mary Pickford in *Such a Little Queen* the same year. Hugh Ford remained at Paramount and eventually was responsible for picture production—assisted by Albert Kaufman—at Famous Players studios in New York. William Sorelle, *the lead,* had been a veteran of the films from the beginning of Thomas A. Edison's film production. He had been acting character parts and leads from the time when the first film stories began to appear.

10. **MICE AND MEN.** *Director,* J. Searle Dawley. Marshall Neilan, *leading man,* was a stage actor and then worked for a time at Biograph, Kalem, and Lasky, playing leading men or character roles. He was lead to Mary Pickford in *Madam Butterfly* at Famous Players in 1915. Neilan turned to directing in 1916 and indicated in his direction a superior visual sense and also displayed a sensitive feeling both for character and for recreating the past. He displayed an acute film sense. He directed Marguerite Clark in *Out of a Clear*

Sky (1918) and in *Three Men and a Girl* (1919). Mary Pickford considered him to be her favorite director. He directed her in *Rebecca of Sunnybrook Farm* (1917), *Stella Maris* (1918), *Daddy Long Legs* (1919), *Dorothy Vernon of Haddon Hall* (1924). He also directed Colleen Moore, Blanche Sweet, and Constance Talmadge. He died in 1958.

11. **OUT OF THE DRIFTS.** *Director,* J. Searle Dawley. The *leading man,* William Courtleigh, Jr., had been a popular figure in Pathé serials, having been co-billed with Lillian Lorraine, a Follies beauty in *Neal of the Navy,* (1915).

12. **MOLLY MAKE-BELIEVE.** *Director,* J. Searle Dawley. *Leading man* Mahlon Hamilton was being featured at Metro in 1918 and was the lead for Mary Pickford in *Daddy Long Legs* in 1919. He was featured in *Little Old New York* with Marion Davies as the star and played the lead for Agnes Ayres in *The Heart Raider* — both films being made in 1923.

13. **SILKS AND SATINS.** *Director,* J. Searle Dawley. Vernon Steele played *lead* roles for World Pictures in 1915, and one of these was *Hearts in Exile* starring Clara Kimball Young. He moved to Lasky (Paramount) before the year was over where he played opposite Ethel Clayton in *For the Defense.* By 1917 he had joined Goldwyn Pictures where he was lead man for Mae Marsh in the company's first picture, *Polly of the Circus.*

14. **LITTLE LADY EILEEN.** *Director,* J. Searle Dawley. *Leading man,* Vernon Steele.

15. **MISS GEORGE WASHINGTON.** *Director,* J. Searle Dawley. Niles Welch was a *leading man* for the Metro film company in 1915. By 1916, he was playing leads for Paramount at its New York Famous Players studio. Welch was still with Paramount in 1919, when he supported Vivian Martin in *Jane Goes A-wooing.* He was filling supporting roles for Realart in 1922.

16. **SNOW WHITE.** *Director,* J. Searle Dawley. Creighton Hale was appearing as a screen lead by 1915, and one of his early roles was that of the leading man to Pearl White in the serial, *The Exploits of Elaine* (Pathé). This was followed by *The Iron Claw,* (Pathé, 1916), another serial in which he supported Pearl White. After appearing in *Snow White,* Hale returned to a lead in a Pathé serial, and then by 1920, he was playing character roles in D. W. Griffith's *Idol Dancer* and *Way Down East.* An actor in demand, he continued playing character roles, leads, and second leads until after the silent era ended. Among his significant roles was that of the lead to Florence Vidor in Ernst Lubitsch's *Marriage Circle* (1924).

17. **THE FORTUNES OF FIFI.** *Director* Robert G. Vignola was hired by the Kalem film company not long after it was founded in 1907, and by 1910, he was one of their leading actors. Like Marshall Neilan, he left acting for directing, and by 1917, he had established a name of significance in the field. In the *Fortunes of Fifi,* he indicated an appreciation of historical authenticity in his preserving of the quaint air of Paris, in the days of Napoleon Bonaparte, with praiseworthy fidelity. Vignola directed both tragedy and comedy well. His *The Knife,* (Select Pictures, 1918) starring Alice Brady, was a tragic, dramatic shocker, while *Experimental Marriage* (1918), made for the same company, was a romantic comedy starring Constance Talmadge. Both pictures displayed maturity in direction. William Sorelle, *leading man,* had been an obscure stage actor when he became the first member of the Edison Stock Company. He was paid $30 a week. More than a decade passed before Sorelle played the lead in *The Fortunes of Fifi.* After this picture, he continued for a time to play film leads.

18. **THE VALENTINE GIRL.** *Director*, J. Searle Dawley. Richard Barthelmess, (1895-1963), appeared in six films starring Marguerite Clark playing the *leading man* in each of them. Barthelmess was born in New York City in 1895 and first received attention in *War Brides* (1916) in which he was featured with Alla Nazimova as star. His romantic qualities and great sensitivity were best displayed in D. W. Griffith's *Broken Blossoms* (1919) and *Way Down East* (1920)—both opposite Lillian Gish. His best starring role in silent films was in *Tolable David* (1921) directed by Henry King. He easily made the transition from silent films to sound where he is well remembered for his starring part in William Dieterle's *The Last Flight* (1932). Later he became an effective character actor, and his last role was in *Desert Fury* (1947).

19. **THE AMAZONS.** The *director* Joseph Kaufman had been a leading actor for the Lubin film company, but he also had done some directing in the early years of the films as well. As a director, he was better known and was established as such at Famous Players in 1917 when *The Amazons* was made. Polish, sophistication, and humor were evident in his direction, making *The Amazons* delightful. Jack Standing, the *leading man*, too had acted for the Lubin company, having played opposite Florence Lawrence in *A Good Turn* in 1911. He was still with Lubin in 1914, but by 1917, he had joined Famous Players. He did not gain the fame of the supporting actor in *The Amazons*, Adolphe Menjou, who would be established as a star in 1923 for his role in *A Woman of Paris* directed by Charlie Chaplin.

20. **BAB'S DIARY.** *Director*, J. Searle Dawley. *Leading man*, Richard Barthelmess.

21. **BAB'S BURGLAR.** *Director*, J. Searle Dawley. *Leading man*, Richard Barthelmess.

22. **BAB'S MATINEE IDOL.** *Director*, J. Searle Dawley. Nigel Barrie, *leading man*, came to Famous Players (Paramount) from the World Film Company, and in 1917, he appeared in two Bab stories with Marguerite Clark and was leading man in *Bab's Matinee Idol*. He was handsome, capable, and played opposite her again in *Widow by Proxy* (1919). He left Paramount for First National and acted as leading man to Constance Talmadge in the clever *East is West* (1922).

23. **THE SEVEN SWANS.** *Director*, J. Searle Dawley. *Leading man*, Richard Barthelmess.

24. **RICH MAN, POOR MAN.** *Director*, J. Searle Dawley. *Leading man*, Richard Barthelmess.

25. **PRUNELLA.** *Director* Maurice Tourneur was born at Paris in 1878, and after studying under Rodin, became an artist. He later turned to acting and eventually to the films. As director for the Éclair company, he came to the United States in 1914 to run Éclair's Tuscon studios. He was an artist on film, and the pictorial quality of his pictures and the clarity with which these stories were told, caused him to be ranked as one of the great directors. High among his prestige films stood *Prunella* and *The Bluebird* (1918). His pictorial style of narrative was evident too in *A Doll's House* (1918), *Treasure Island* (1920), *The Last of the Mohicans (1922), The Christian* (1923), *Never the Twain Shall Meet* (1924), and *Aloma of the South Seas* (1926). He returned to France in 1927 and continued directing films of unusual quality until 1949. He died in 1961. Jules Raucourt, *leading man*, appeared in a character role in *The Seven Swans*, and Marguerite Clark, seeing his potentialities, chose him for the part of Pierrot in *Prunella*. That same year, 1918, he also played lead to Pauline Frederick in *La Tosca* (Paramount).

26. **UNCLE TOM'S CABIN.** *Director,* J. Searle Dawley. Frank Losee, popular character actor of Paramount Pictures, played the role of Uncle Tom. There was no leading man. Losee was kept busy between 1915-1918 playing character roles for Hazel Dawn, Pauline Frederick, Mary Pickford, and Marguerite Clark.

27. **OUT OF A CLEAR SKY.** *Director,* Marshall Neilan. Thomas Meighan, *the leading man,* grew in popular demand from 1915 when he played lead with Blanche Sweet and Charlotte Walker at Paramount to 1918 when he played opposite Mary Pickford in *M'liss* (1918). Then in 1919 stardom came after he appeared in *Male and Female* directed by Cecil B. DeMille and *The Miracle Man* directed by George Loane Tucker. Meighan's popularity continued all through the 1920's. Critics of the film seem to ignore him, but he is still remembered by that portion yet remaining of those millions of movie goers who once visited the box office often enough to make him a star.

28. **LITTLE MISS HOOVER.** John S. Robertson *directed* Marguerite Clark with skill and sensitivity, preserving a joyous mood in *Little Miss Hoover* (1918), *Let's Elope* (1919), and *Come Out of the Kitchen* (1919). There was a touch of genius evident in his direction of John Barrymore in *Dr. Jekyll and Mr. Hyde* (Paramount, 1920). It was a powerful and effective film with good make-up of Barrymore as Hyde. Robertson was adept too in directing sound pictures, and his *The Greatest Gamble,* starring Richard Dix (RKO, 1934) indicated that the talents he had acquired in the silent days had been enhanced. Eugene O'Brien, the *leading man* came from the New York stage to the screen and appeared on Broadway as leading man to Ethel Barrymore, Irene Fenwick, and others. The Essanay film company brought him to the screen in 1916 and by the next year, he was playing opposite Norma Talmadge in *The Safety Curtain* for Select Pictures. In 1918, he moved to Paramount to play leads to Elsie Ferguson and Marguerite Clark.

O'Brien became a star for Myron Selznick of the Selznick film organization in 1919, but he was once more playing leads to Norma Talmadge at First National in 1922. O'Brien went back to the stage in 1923 to star on Broadway in *Steve.*

29. **MRS. WIGGS OF THE CABBAGE PATCH.** Hugh Ford, *director.* Gareth Hughes, *leading man,* gained some attention on the stage in *Moloch* (1915) and *The Guilty Man* (1916). He turned to the screen by 1919, appearing in the cast of *Eyes of Youth* (Equity) which starred Clara Kimball Young and introduced Rudolph Valentino as a lead. That same year Hughes went to Paramount where he gained fame in 1921 for his superior performance of Tommy in J.M. Barrie's *Sentimental Tommy* with May McAvoy, a picture brilliantly directed by John S. Robertson. Hughes, May McAvoy, Bert Lytell and Betty Compson all received favorable attention for their performances in *Kick In* (Paramount, 1922). Hughes returned to the stage where he starred in *The Dunce* in 1925.

30. **THREE MEN AND A GIRL.** Marshall Neilan, *director. Leading man,* Richard Barthelmess.

31. **LET'S ELOPE.** John S. Robertson, *director. Leading man,* Frank Mills was playing lead roles as early as 1901 when he appeared opposite Elise de Wolfe in *The Way of the World* on the New York stage. By 1917, he was in Pathé pictures as a leading man to Florence Reed in *Today.* He soon changed to Paramount Pictures, and in 1919, he played the lead to Marguerite Clark in *Let's Elope* and to Billie Burke in *The Misleading Widow.*

32. **COME OUT OF THE KITCHEN.** John S. Robertson, *director.* Eugene O'Brien, *leading man.*

33. **GIRLS.** Walter Edwards, *director,* established a favorable reputation as a director of domestic comedies and romantic farces. Constance Talmadge valued his work so much that she obtained his services to direct nine of the sixteen films she made for Select. Marguerite Clark, adept at comedy, turned to him to

direct her last six pictures. *Leading man* Harrison Ford possessed a flair for sophisticated comedy that kept him in constant demand. He gave a sincere, polished touch to everything he did. He was an excellent lead to Marguerite Clark in *Girls* and in *Easy to Get* (1920). Harrison Ford was one of the many screen performers who came from the New York stage, but his success was much greater on the screen. He played leads to Constance Talmadge in twelve romantic comedies. He was also leading man to Norma Talmadge, Vivian Martin, Lila Lee, Marion Davies and others. He played character roles too and was active all through the silent film era. He died in 1957 at seventy-three.

34. **WIDOW BY PROXY.** Walter Edwards, *director.* Nigel Barrie, *leading man.*

35. **LUCK IN PAWN.** Walter Edwards, *director. Leading man* Charles Meredith filled his role adequately in *Luck in Pawn.* He had all of the looks needed to play leads, and he continued for a time in such roles in silent pictures. He was opposite Blanche Sweet in *Simple Souls* (Pathé, 1920) and Katherine McDonald in *The Beautiful Liar* (First National, 1921).

36. **A GIRL NAMED MARY.** Walter Edwards, *director. Leading man* Wallace MacDonald had played leads for Triangle Pictures, one of them being opposite Alma Rubens in *Madam Sphynx* (1918). After Triangle folded, he was with Vitagraph briefly and then went to Goldwyn where he was with Mae Marsh in *Spotlight Sadie* (1919). He was leading man at Paramount before the end of 1919. Later Wallace MacDonald joined First National where he played a character role to Milton Sills in *The Sea Hawk* (1924) and the lead to Norma Talmadge in *The Lady* (1925). He was with Universal by 1926.

37. **ALL-OF-A-SUDDEN PEGGY.** Walter Edwards, *director.* Jack Mulhall, *leading man,* played in over a hundred films in his long career and was lead and star too in silent pictures. He was successful as well in

sound films. One of his first featured roles of importance was in *Sirens of the Sea* (Universal, 1917) with Louise Lovely and Carmel Myers. The next year he was lead to Mabel Normand in *Mickey* (Mabel Normand Feature Film Co., 1918), a film made popular by a best selling song written about the story. Mulhall had a youthful, likeable charm that fitted him for romantic comedies. Among his other leading women of the silent films were Enid Bennett, Constance Talmadge, Viola Dana, and Dorothy Mackaill. He moved easily from silent to talking pictures and was the first male lead to earn a $1,000 a week. Jack Mulhall died on June 1, 1979 at 92.

38. **EASY TO GET.** Walter Edwards, *director.* Harrison Ford, leading man.

39. **SCRAMBLED WIVES.** *Director* Edward H. Griffith first gained attention during World War I for his propaganda films for the United States government. He was directing films in 1921 for Realart when Marguerite Clark chose him for her independent production of *Scrambled Wives.* That same year, he directed Alice Brady in a melodrama titled *Dawn of the East* for Realart (Paramount). Leon P. (Pierre) Gendron was a satisfactory *lead* in *Scrambled Wives.* He had the essential good looks and a sense for farce required for the part. He was still playing leading men roles in 1925 when he appeared opposite Evelyn Brent in *The Dangerous Flirt* (FBO).

The bibliography for the motion pictures of Marguerite Clark consists of Blum, Daniel, *A Pictorial History of the American Theatre.* New York: Bonanza Books, 1960; Blum, Daniel, *A Pictorial History of the Silent Screen.* New York: Grosset and Dunlap, 1953; Bodeen, De Witt, *From Hollywood.* New York: A. S. Barnes and Co., London: Tantivy Press, 1976; Lasky, Jesse, *I Blow My Own Horn.* Garden City, New York: Doubleday and Co., 1957; *The Moving Picture World* (1915-1921); *Motion Picture News* (1916-1917).

Index